The Original
Summer Bridge Activities™

Bridging Grades Kindergarten to First

We're so glad you decided to join us on a fun-filled summer learning adventure. Be sure to access your FREE Summer Bridge Activities™ online companion.

Here's how:

Step 1: Visit **www.summerlearningactivities.com/sba**

Step 2: Register your Summer Bridge Activities™ book

Step 3: Download the FREE Summer Bridge Activities™ mobile apps

---

Summer Bridge Activities™
online companion

Welcome, My account settings	Log out

Welcome to Summer Bridge Activities! We're so glad you decided to join us on a fun-filled summer learning adventure. To get the most out of your online companion click here for tips and frequently asked questions.

Child 1   Add Child ➕

Child 1   Update Child's Password

Bridging Grades K to 1

Assessments

Focused Practice Workbooks

Incentive Contracts

Family Fun

Mobile Apps

Preview Games

Caution: Exercise activities may require adult supervision. Before beginning any exercise activity, consult a physician. Written parental permission is suggested for those using this book in group situations. Children should always warm up prior to beginning any exercise activity and should stop immediately if they feel any discomfort during exercise.

Caution: Before beginning any food activity, ask parents' permission and inquire about the child's food allergies and religious or other food restrictions.

Caution: Nature activities may require adult supervision. Before beginning any nature activity, ask parents' permission and inquire about the child's plant and animal allergies. Remind the child not to touch plants or animals during the activity without adult supervision.

The authors and publisher are not responsible or liable for any injury that may result from performing the exercises or activities in this book.

Credits

Series Creator: Michele D. Van Leeuwen

Content Editor: JulieAnna Kirsch

Copy Editor: Barrie Hoople

Layout and Cover Design: Chasity Rice

Cover Art: Robbie Short

ISBN 978-1-60418-818-9

02-061121151

© Carson-Dellosa

Table of Contents

About Summer Learning

Dear Parents:

Did you know that many children experience learning loss when they do not engage in educational activities during the summer? This means that some of what they have spent time learning over the preceding school year evaporates during the summer months. However, summer learning loss is something that you can help prevent. Below are a few suggestions for fun and engaging activities that can help children maintain and grow their academic skills during the summer.

- Read with your child every day. Visit your local library together and select books on subjects that interest your child.

- Ask your child's teacher to recommend books for summer reading.

- Explore parks, nature preserves, museums, and cultural centers.

- Consider every day as a day full of teachable moments. Measuring ingredients for recipes and reviewing maps before a car trip are ways to learn or reinforce skills.

- Each day, set goals for your child to accomplish. For example, complete five math problems or read one section or chapter in a book.

- Encourage your child to complete the activities in books such as Summer Bridge Activities™ to help bridge the summer learning gap.

To learn more about summer learning loss and summer learning programs, visit *www.summerlearning.org.*

Have a memorable summer!

Brenda McLaughlin and Sarah Pitcock
National Summer Learning Association

About Summer Bridge Activities™

Summer Bridge Activities™: Bridging Grades Kindergarten to First helps prepare your rising first grader for a successful school year. The activities in this book are designed to review the skills that your child mastered in kindergarten, preview the skills that he or she will learn in first grade, and help prevent summer learning loss. No matter how wonderful your child's classroom experiences are, your involvement outside of the classroom is crucial to his or her academic success. Together with *Summer Bridge Activities™: Bridging Grades Kindergarten to First*, you can fill the summer months with learning experiences that will deepen and enrich your child's knowledge and prepare your child for the upcoming school year.

Summer Bridge Activities™ is the original workbook series developed to help parents support their children academically during the summer months. While many other summer workbook series are available, Summer Bridge Activities™ continues to be the series that teachers recommend most.

The three sections in this workbook correspond to the three months of traditional summer vacation. Each section begins with a goal-setting activity, a word list, and information for parents about the fitness and character development activities located throughout the section.

To achieve maximum results, your child should complete two activity pages each day. Activities cover a range of subjects, including phonics, handwriting, addition and subtraction, time and money, shapes and colors, character development, and fitness. These age-appropriate activities are presented in a fun and creative way to challenge and engage your child. Each activity page is numbered by day, and each day includes a space for your child to place a colorful, motivational sticker after he or she completes the day's activities.

Bonus extension activities that encourage outdoor learning, science experiments, and social studies exercises are located at the end of each section. Complete these activities with your child throughout each month as time allows.

An answer key located at the end of the book allows you to check your child's work. The included flash cards help reinforce basic skills, and a certificate of completion will help you and your child celebrate his or her summer learning success!

Skills Matrix

Day	Addition	Alphabet	Character Development	Colors	Fine Motor Skills	Fitness	Geometry & Measurement	Grammar & Language Arts	Graphing & Probability	Handwriting	Numbers & Counting	Patterns	Phonics	Puzzles & Games	Reading Comprehension	Science	Shape Recognition	Social Studies	Subtraction	Time & Money	Visual Discrimination
1		★					★														
2					★					★			★								
3										★			★								★
4										★			★								★
5						★				★	★		★								
6		★								★	★		★								
7		★								★	★		★								
8										★	★	★	★				★				
9		★								★			★						★		
10		★								★			★						★		
11									★	★	★		★								
12										★	★		★								
13								★		★	★		★								
14					★					★	★		★								★
15						★				★	★		★								
16							★			★	★		★								
17				★						★			★							★	
18				★						★			★							★	
19				★						★			★							★	
20			★							★	★		★								
BONUS PAGES!		★														★		★			★
1	★				★					★			★								
2	★					★				★			★								
3	★									★			★				★				
4										★			★								★
5			★										★		★						
6				★									★		★				★		
7										★		★	★						★		
8										★			★						★		
9													★						★		★
10				★							★		★			★					
11							★			★			★								

vi

© Carson-Dellosa

Skills Matrix

Day	Addition	Alphabet	Character Development	Colors	Fine Motor Skills	Fitness	Geometry & Measurement	Grammar & Language Arts	Graphing & Probability	Handwriting	Numbers & Counting	Patterns	Phonics	Puzzles & Games	Reading Comprehension	Science	Shape Recognition	Social Studies	Subtraction	Time & Money	Visual Discrimination
12							★				★		★								
13													★								★
14										★	★		★						★		
15								★					★	★							
16								★					★								★
17				★		★					★		★		★						
18								★		★			★	★							
19											★		★								
20											★		★							★	
									BONUS PAGES!							★		★			★
1	★										★		★		★				★		
2											★		★							★	
3						★					★		★								
4											★		★			★					
5											★		★		★					★	
6											★		★								★
7											★		★							★	
8	★	★													★						
9	★												★	★							
10								★					★						★		
11													★						★		
12	★												★		★				★		
13	★						★						★						★		
14	★												★						★		
15			★							★			★								
16	★								★				★						★		
17										★			★								
18	★									★					★					★	
19						★		★					★							★	
20					★								★								
			★					★		BONUS PAGES!				★			★	★			

Encouraging Summer Reading

Literacy is the single most important skill that your child needs to be successful in school. The following list includes ideas of ways that you can help your child discover the great adventures of reading!

- Establish a time for reading each day. Ask your child about what he or she is reading. Try to relate the material to an event that is happening this summer or to another book or story.

- Let your child see you reading for enjoyment. Talk about the great things that you discover when you read.

- Create a summer reading list. Choose books from the reading list (pages ix–x) or head to the library and explore the shelves. A general rule for selecting books at the appropriate reading level is to choose a page and ask your child to read it aloud. If he or she does not know more than five words on the page, the book may be too difficult.

- Read newspaper and magazine articles, recipes, menus, maps, and street signs on a daily basis to show your child the importance of reading.

- Find books that relate to your child's experiences. For example, if you are going camping, find a book about camping. This will help your child develop new interests.

- Visit the library each week. Let your child choose his or her own books, but do not hesitate to ask your librarian for suggestions. Often, librarians can recommend books based on what your child enjoyed in the past.

- Make up stories. This is especially fun to do in the car, on camping trips, or while waiting at the airport. Encourage your child to tell a story with a beginning, a middle, and an end. Or, have your child start a story and let other family members build on it.

- Encourage your child to join a summer reading club at the library or a local bookstore. Your child may enjoy talking to other children about the books that he or she has read.

Summer Reading List

The summer reading list includes fiction and nonfiction titles. Experts recommend that parents read to kindergarten and first-grade children for at least 10 to 15 minutes each day. Then, ask questions about the story to reinforce comprehension.

Decide on an amount of daily reading time for each month. You may want to write the time on each Monthly Goals page at the beginning of each section.

Fiction

Allard, Harry
Miss Nelson Is Missing!

Banks, Kate
Max's Words

Berenstain, Stan and Jan
The Berenstain Bears Go to School

Berger, Carin
The Little Yellow Leaf

Brett, Jan
Goldilocks and the Three Bears

Carle, Eric
The Mixed-Up Chameleon
The Very Quiet Cricket

Curtis, Jamie Lee
Is There Really a Human Race?
*Today I Feel Silly & Other Moods That
    Make My Day*

Demi
The Empty Pot

Falconer, Ian
Olivia

Fox, Mem
A Particular Cow

Gilman, Phoebe
Jillian Jiggs

Harris, Jim
Three Little Dinosaurs

Henkes, Kevin
Chrysanthemum
Lilly's Purple Plastic Purse

Hoberman, Mary Ann
A House Is a House for Me

Krauss, Ruth
The Carrot Seed

Leaf, Munro
The Story of Ferdinand

McCloud, Carol
*Have You Filled a Bucket Today?: A Guide
    to Daily Happiness for Kids*

Piper, Watty
The Little Engine That Could

Priceman, Marjorie
How to Make an Apple Pie and See the World

Summer Reading List (continued)

Fiction (continued)

Rohmann, Eric
My Friend Rabbit

Rylant, Cynthia
Night in the Country
The Relatives Came

Seeger, Laura Vaccaro
First the Egg

Sendak, Maurice
In the Night Kitchen
Where the Wild Things Are

Seuss, Dr.
Oh, the Thinks You Can Think!
The Shape of Me and Other Stuff

Silverstein, Shel
A Giraffe and a Half
The Giving Tree

Slobodkina, Esphyr
Caps for Sale

Waber, Bernard
Ira Sleeps Over

Walsh, Ellen Stoll
Mouse Paint

Whybrow, Ian
Harry and the Bucketful of Dinosaurs
    (formerly *Sammy and the Dinosaurs*)

Willems, Mo
Don't Let the Pigeon Stay Up Late!
Knuffle Bunny: A Cautionary Tale

Yolen, Jane
How Do Dinosaurs Say Goodnight?

Nonfiction

Branley, Franklyn M.
What Makes a Magnet?

Burns, Marilyn
The Greedy Triangle

Ehlert, Lois
Waiting for Wings

Gerstein, Mordicai
The Man Who Walked Between the Towers

Gray, Samantha
Eye Wonder: Birds

Lauber, Patricia
Be a Friend to Trees

Martin, Jacqueline Briggs
Snowflake Bentley

Musgrove, Margaret
Ashanti to Zulu: African Traditions

Page, Robin
What Do You Do with a Tail Like This?

Schwartz, David M.
If You Hopped Like a Frog

Monthly Goals

A *goal* is something that you want to accomplish. Sometimes, reaching a goal can be hard work!

Think of three goals to set for yourself this month. For example, you may want to exercise for 10 minutes each day. Have an adult help you write your goals on the lines.

Place a sticker next to each goal that you complete. Feel proud that you have met your goals!

1. _____ PLACE STICKER HERE

2. _____ PLACE STICKER HERE

3. _____ PLACE STICKER HERE

Word List

The following words are used in this section. They are good words for you to know. Read each word aloud with an adult. When you see a word from this list on a page, circle it with your favorite color of crayon.

animal   number

color   practice

different   set

letter   shape

lowercase   uppercase

Introduction to Flexibility

This section includes fitness and character development activities that focus on flexibility. These activities are designed to get your child moving and to get her thinking about building her physical fitness and her character.

Physical Flexibility

Flexibility to the average person means being able to accomplish everyday physical tasks easily, like bending to tie a shoe. These everyday tasks can be difficult for people whose muscles and joints have not been used and stretched regularly.

Proper stretching allows muscles and joints to move through their full range of motion, which is key to maintaining good flexibility. There are many ways that your child stretches every day without realizing it. She may reach for a dropped pencil or a box of cereal on the top shelf. Point out these examples to your child and explain why good flexibility is important to her health and growth. Challenge her to improve her flexibility consciously. Encourage her to set a stretching goal for the summer, such as practicing daily until she can touch her toes.

Flexibility of Character

While it is important to have a flexible body, it is also important to be mentally flexible. Share with your child that being mentally flexible means being open minded. Talk about how disappointing it can be when things do not go her way and explain that disappointment is a normal reaction. Give a recent example of when unforeseen circumstances ruined her plans, such as having a trip to the park canceled because of rain. Explain that there will be situations in life when unexpected things happen. Often, it is how a person reacts to those circumstances that affects the outcome. By using relatable examples, you can arm your child with tools to be flexible, such as having realistic expectations, brainstorming solutions to make a disappointing situation better, and looking for good things that may have resulted from the initial disappointment.

Mental flexibility can take many forms. For example, respecting the differences of other children, sharing, and taking turns are ways that your child can practice flexibility. Encourage your child to be flexible and praise her when you see her exhibiting this important character trait.

Track your growth this summer. Have an adult help you measure your height and weight. Fill in the blanks. Draw and color the picture to look like you.

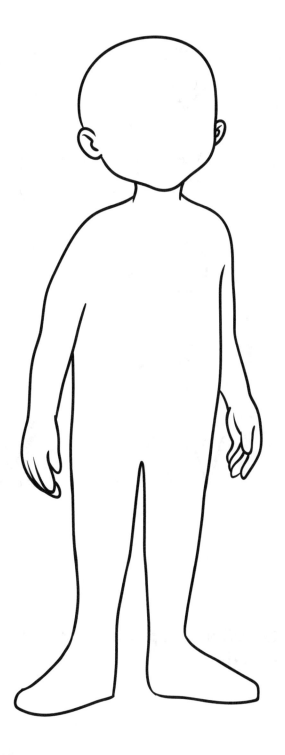

Your Height:

_____

Your Weight:

_____

DAY 1

Say the alphabet in order. Touch each letter as you say it.

Aa Bb Cc Dd

Ee Ff Gg Hh

Ii Jj Kk Ll

Mm Nn Oo Pp

Qq Rr Ss Tt

Uu Vv Ww Xx

Yy Zz

Ask an adult to say a letter. Find the letter and put a marker on it. Keep going until you have covered every letter.

PLACE
STICKER
HERE

Trace and write the numbers 0, 1, 2, and 3.

0 0

1 1

2 2

3 3

Trace the lines to help the animals find their homes.

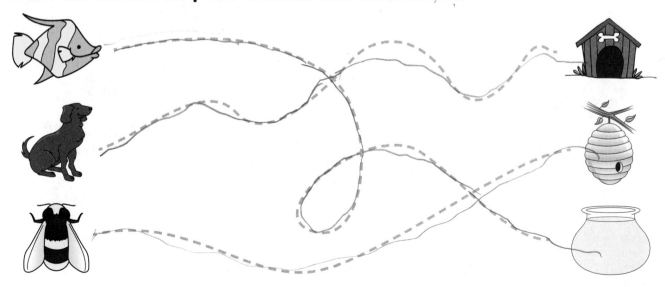

DAY 2

Baseball begins with the /b/ sound. Practice writing uppercase and lowercase **B**s.

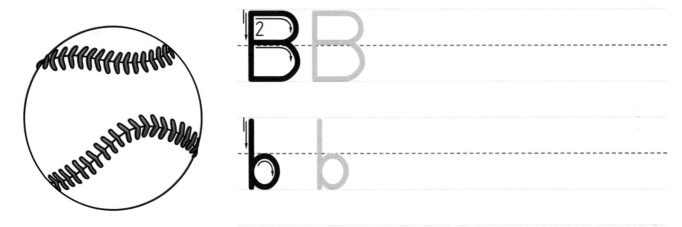

Say the name of each picture. Circle each picture that begins with the /b/ sound, like *baseball*.

FACTOID: Most baseballs have 108 stitches.

Trace and write the numbers 4, 5, 6, and 7.

Circle the object in each box that is different.

1.
2.
3.
4.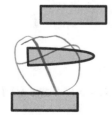
5.
6.

DAY 3

Cake begins with the hard *c* sound. Practice writing uppercase and lowercase Cs.

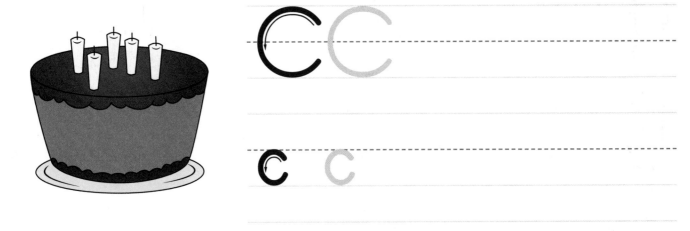

Say the name of each picture. Circle each picture that begins with the hard *c* sound, like *cake*.

FITNESS FLASH: Touch your toes 10 times.

* See page ii.

PLACE STICKER HERE

Trace and write the numbers 8, 9, and 10.

Complete each shape to match the first shape in each row.

1.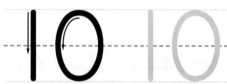

2.

3.

DAY 4

Duck begins with the /d/ sound. Practice writing uppercase and lowercase Ds.

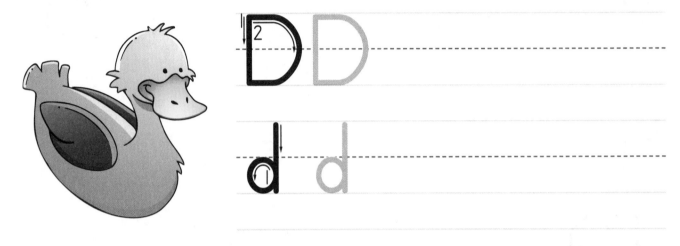

Say the name of each picture. Circle each picture that begins with the /d/ sound, like *duck*.

FACTOID: Ducks stay dry in the water because their feathers are waterproof.

PLACE STICKER HERE

Count the animals on the farm. Color one box for each animal you count.

The Farmyard Stretch

Choose your favorite farm animal. Imagine how the animal stretches.
Practice stretching like the farm animal. Then, show your family and
friends. Can they guess the farm animal that you chose?

* See page ii.

DAY 5

Fish begins with the /f/ sound. Practice writing uppercase and lowercase Fs.

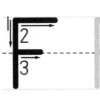

Say the name of each picture. Circle each picture that begins with the /f/ sound, like *fish*.

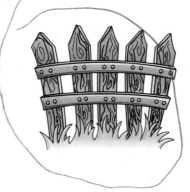

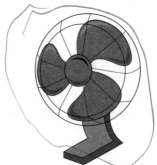

 FITNESS FLASH: Practice a V-sit. Stretch three times.

* See page ii.

PLACE STICKER HERE

Say each number. Color the number of boxes to match the number.

6									
7									
8									
9									
10									

Write the missing lowercase letters.

a, b, ___, ___, e, ___, g, ___, i, ___,

k, ___, ___, n, o, ___, q, ___, ___,

___, u, v, ___, ___, ___, z

DAY 6

Girl begins with the /g/ sound. Practice writing uppercase and lowercase **G**s.

Say the name of each picture. Circle each picture that begins with the /g/ sound, like *girl*.

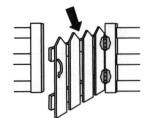

CHARACTER CHECK: With an adult, look up the word *caring* in the dictionary. Talk about a time when you were caring.

PLACE
STICKER
HERE

Count the number of objects in each set. Write the number on the line.

1.

2.

_____

3.
_____

4.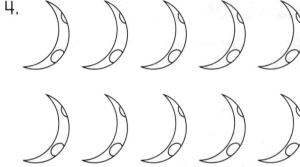
_____

Write the missing uppercase letters.

A, B, ___, ___, E, ___, ___, H, ___,

___, ___, ___, M, ___, ___, ___, Q,

___, S, ___, ___, ___, W, ___, ___, Z

DAY 7

Horse begins with the /h/ sound. Practice writing uppercase and lowercase Hs.

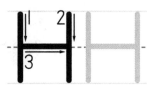

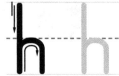

Say the name of each picture. Circle each picture that begins with the /h/ sound, like *horse*.

FACTOID: A horse cannot see what is directly in front of its face.

PLACE STICKER HERE

Draw the correct number of shapes in each box.

1.	2.
8 circles	4 rectangles
3.	4.
5 squares	7 ovals

Draw the shape that comes next in each pattern.

5.   _____

6.   _____

7.   _____

DAY 8

Jack-in-the-box begins with the /j/ sound. Practice writing uppercase and lowercase Js.

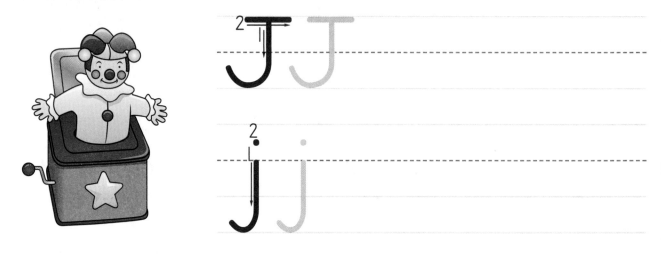

Say the name of each picture. Circle each picture that begins with the /j/ sound, like *jack-in-the-box*.

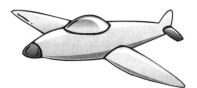

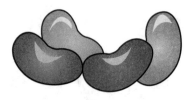

FITNESS FLASH: Do 10 shoulder shrugs.

* See page ii.

PLACE STICKER HERE

Color each circle red. Color each square blue.

Draw a line to match each uppercase letter to its lowercase letter.

A	c	G	g
B	a	H	l
C	f	I	j
D	d	J	h
E	e	K	i
F	b	L	k

DAY 9

Kangaroo begins with the /k/ sound. Practice writing uppercase and lowercase **K**s.

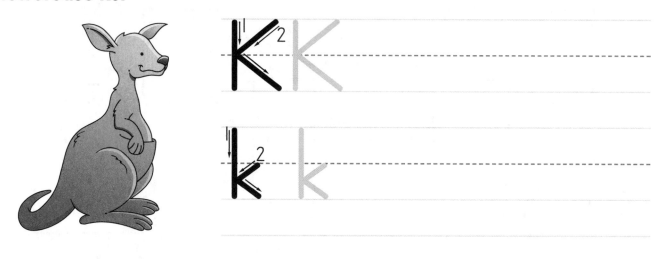

Say the name of each picture. Circle each picture that begins with the /k/ sound, like *kangaroo*.

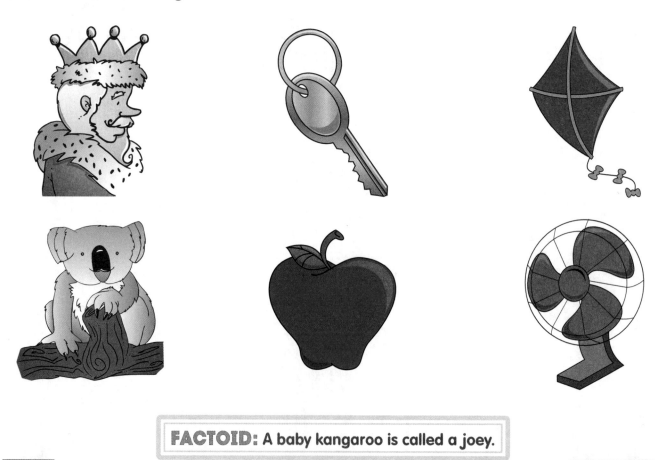

FACTOID: A baby kangaroo is called a joey.

PLACE
STICKER
HERE

Color each triangle yellow. Color each rectangle green.

Draw a line to match each uppercase letter to its lowercase letter.

M	p	T	u
N	m	U	t
O	q	V	v
P	r	W	x
Q	s	X	z
R	n	Y	y
S	o	Z	w

DAY 10

Ladybug begins with the /l/ sound. Practice writing uppercase and lowercase **L**s.

Say the name of each picture. Circle each picture that begins with the /l/ sound, like *ladybug*.

 FITNESS FLASH: Do arm circles for 30 seconds.

* See page ii.

PLACE STICKER HERE

Write the next number in each set.

1.
| 7 | 8 | |

2.
| 2 | 3 | |

3.
| 14 | 15 | |

4.
| 18 | 19 | |

Neyla saw 5 monkeys, 1 elephant, 4 lions, and 2 bears at the zoo. Color the graph to show the number of each animal that Neyla saw.

Animals at the Zoo

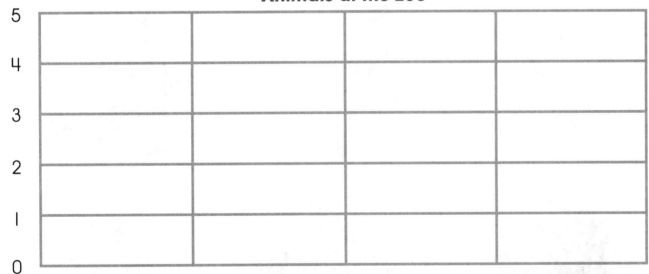

5.   Neyla saw more _____ than any other animal.

DAY 11

Mouse begins with the /m/ sound. Practice writing uppercase and lowercase Ms.

Say the name of each picture. Circle each picture that begins with the /m/ sound, like *mouse*.

CHARACTER CHECK: Think of a time when you did something nice for a friend or family member. How did that make you feel?

PLACE
STICKER
HERE

Write the first number in each set.

1.

2 3

2.
6 7

3.
12 13

4.
19 20

Follow the directions to complete each problem.

5.   Start at the left. Circle the animal that is third.

6.   Start at the left. Draw a rectangle around the animal that is second.

7.   Start at the left. Draw a triangle around the animal that is last.

DAY 12

Nest begins with the /n/ sound. Practice writing uppercase and lowercase Ns.

Say the name of each picture. Circle each picture that begins with the /n/ sound, like *nest*.

FACTOID: A hummingbird's nest is about the size of a walnut.

PLACE STICKER HERE

Color the first race car blue. Color the second race car green. Color the third race car orange.

A *noun* is a word that names a person, a place, or a thing. Circle the people. Draw Xs on the places. Draw squares around the things.

girl   school   pencil

farm   baby   desk

DAY 13

Parrot begins with the /p/ sound. Practice writing uppercase and lowercase **P**s.

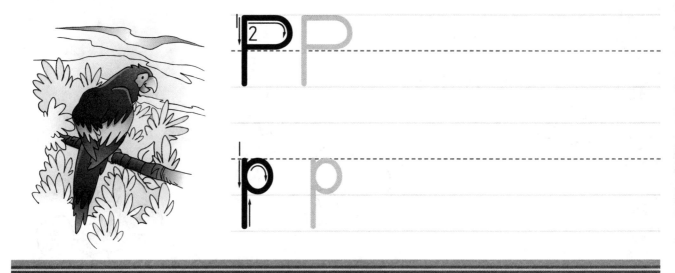

Say the name of each picture. Circle each picture that begins with the /p/ sound, like *parrot*.

FITNESS FLASH: Do 10 shoulder shrugs.

* See page ii.

PLACE
STICKER
HERE

Circle the bowl with more fish.

1.

Circle the plate with fewer cookies.

2.

Draw a line to help the mouse find the cheese.

DAY 14

Queen begins with the /kw/ sound. Practice writing uppercase and lowercase Qs.

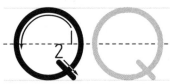

Say the name of each picture. Circle each picture that begins with the /kw/ sound, like *queen*.

FACTOID: The Imperial State Crown of England has more than 3,000 gems.

Circle the set with more objects.

1.

Circle the set with fewer objects.

2.

Animal Antics

Stretching exercises will help improve your flexibility. Try the stretch shown on the right. As you stretch, pretend that you are a flexible flamingo. Use your imagination, and you may even forget that you are stretching!

* See page ii.

DAY 15

Rug begins with the /r/ sound. Practice writing uppercase and lowercase **R**s.

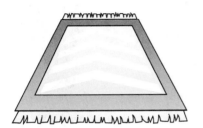

Say the name of each picture. Circle each picture that begins with the /r/ sound, like *rug*.

 **FITNESS FLASH:** Do arm circles for 30 seconds.

* See page ii.

32

PLACE STICKER HERE

Write the missing numbers.

1	2	3	4	5
6	7	8	9	10
11	12	13	14	15
16	17	18	19	20
				25

Draw the other half of the balloon. Color the balloon.

DAY 16

Sandwich begins with the /s/ sound. Practice writing uppercase and lowercase **S**s.

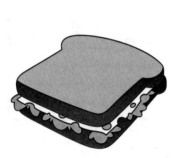

S S

s s

Say the name of each picture. Circle each picture that begins with the /s/ sound, like *sandwich*.

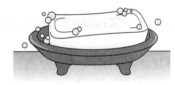

CHARACTER CHECK: Think of two ways that you can be a good friend to someone.

PLACE STICKER HERE

Write the missing numbers on the clock. Then, write the time shown.

_____ : _____

Trace and write each color word. Color each picture the matching color.

red

blue

yellow

DAY 17

Turkey begins with the /t/ sound. Practice writing uppercase and lowercase Ts.

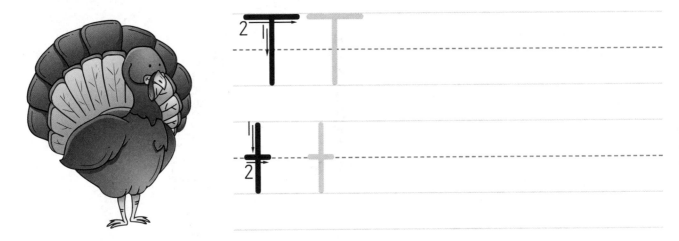

Say the name of each picture. Circle each picture that begins with the /t/ sound, like *turkey*.

FACTOID: An adult turkey can have more than 3,500 feathers.

PLACE
STICKER
HERE

Draw a minute and an hour hand on each clock to show the correct time.

time that I wake up

time that I go to bed

Trace and write each color word. Color each picture the matching color.

orange

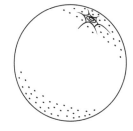

green

purple

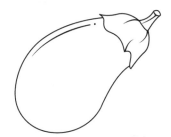

DAY 18

Vacuum begins with the /v/ sound. Practice writing uppercase and lowercase **V**s.

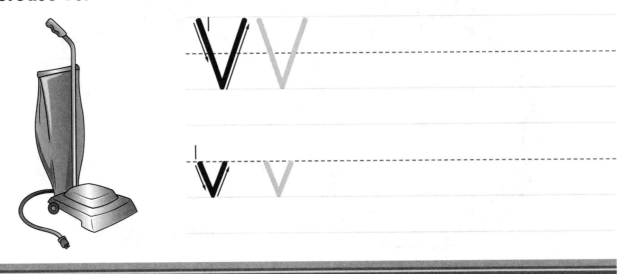

Say the name of each picture. Circle each picture that begins with the /v/ sound, like *vacuum*.

FITNESS FLASH: Touch your toes 10 times.

* See page ii.

PLACE
STICKER
HERE

Look at each clock. Write the time shown.

___ : ___   ___ : ___   ___ : ___

Trace and write each color word. Color each picture the matching color.

black --

violet --

brown ---

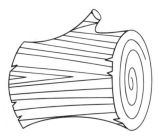

DAY 19

Wig begins with the /w/ sound. Practice writing uppercase and lowercase Ws.

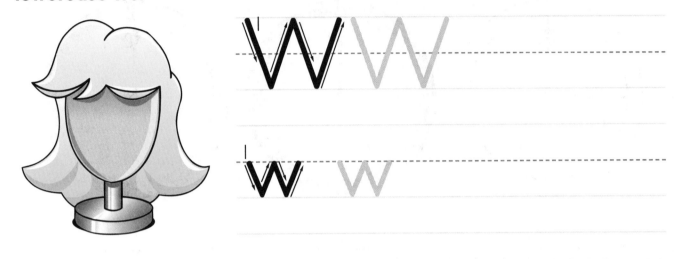

Say the name of each picture. Circle each picture that begins with the /w/ sound, like *wig*.

FACTOID: A walrus's tusks can grow up to three feet long.

PLACE STICKER HERE

Color the numbers in order from 1–10 to help the monkey find the bananas.

Sharing Success

Show the rewards of sharing. On a separate sheet of paper, draw a picture of a monkey sharing her bananas with two friends. Think about what the monkey and her friends look like as they share the bananas. Are they smiling? Do they look like they are getting along?

DAY 20

Fox ends with the /ks/ sound. Practice writing uppercase and lowercase Xs.

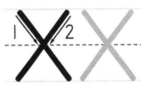

Say the name of each picture. Circle each picture that has the /ks/ sound, like *fox*.

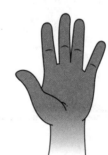

 FITNESS FLASH: Practice a V-sit. Stretch three times.

* See page ii.

PLACE STICKER HERE

Wind Direction

Can bubbles be used to find wind direction?

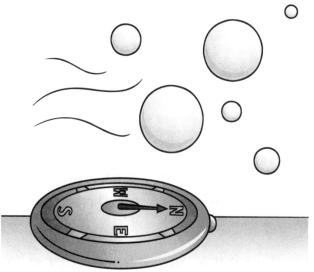

Materials:
- 6 cups (1.4 L) water
- $\frac{3}{4}$ cup (180 mL) light corn syrup
- 2 cups (0.5 L) dishwashing liquid
- jar with lid
- large plastic container
- compass
- bubble wand

Procedure:

Have an adult help you measure and pour the water, light corn syrup, and dishwashing liquid into the jar. Cover the jar and shake it. Let the bubbles settle for about four hours.

After the bubble solution has settled, pour it into the large plastic container. Go outside. Have an adult help you use the compass to find north, south, east, and west. Dip the bubble wand into the solution and blow bubbles upward. Watch to see in which direction the wind blows the bubbles.

1. Circle the direction in which the bubbles moved.

   north   south   east   west

2. Circle the direction from which the wind is blowing.

   north   south   east   west

3. What other things outside show from which direction the wind is blowing?

BONUS

Staying Cool

How can you stay cool in the summer?

Materials:
- fan
- sheet of paper towel
- water

Procedure:

Ask an adult to turn on the fan. Move in front of the fan. Then, move away from the fan. Repeat several times to feel the difference. Think about what the air feels like.

Next, wet the paper towel. Place it on your arm. Move in front of the fan. Then, move away from the fan. Repeat several times to feel the difference.

1. Circle which felt cooler.

    A. moving in front of the fan

    B. moving away from the fan

2. Circle which felt cooler.

    A. moving in front of the fan

    B. moving in front of the fan with the wet paper towel on your arm

3. Write two things that would help keep you cool in the summer.

    _____

    _____

4. On another sheet of paper, draw a picture that shows how you stay cool on a hot summer day.

Being a Good Citizen

A good citizen helps the community, protects the environment, follows rules, and treats others with respect. Circle the two pictures that show children being good citizens.

Draw and color a picture that shows how you are a good citizen.

BONUS

Then and Now

Look at the pictures. Circle each picture that shows something from the present. Draw an X on each picture that shows something from the past.

Community Helpers

Look at each picture. Draw a line to match each community helper to the correct tool.

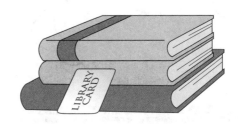

2+1=3   2+2=4
5+2=7   4+2=6
3+2=5   2+3=5
2+4=6   1+2=3

2+2=4
4+2=6
2+3=5
1+2=3

BONUS

Take It Outside!

Look at the picture of a rainbow. Go outside with an adult and try to find one object for each color in the rainbow.

- red
- orange
- yellow
- green
- blue
- indigo
- violet

With an adult, find an animal to watch outdoors, such as a frog or squirrel. Do not get too close! Watch how the animal moves. Then, try to move like the animal. Can you do it?

Read the scavenger hunt list. Go outside with an adult. Try to find one object that matches each description.

Scavenger Hunt List

- something wet
- something scratchy
- something soft
- something slimy
- something pretty

- something dry
- something from a tree
- something tall
- something hard
- something blue

* See page ii.

48

Monthly Goals

Think of three goals that you would like to set for yourself this month. For example, you may want to spend more time reading with your family. Have an adult help you write your goals on the lines.

Place a sticker next to each goal that you complete. Feel proud that you have met your goals!

1. _____ PLACE STICKER HERE

2. _____ PLACE STICKER HERE

3. _____ PLACE STICKER HERE

Word List

The following words are used in this section. They are good words for you to know. Read each word aloud with an adult. When you see a word from this list on a page, circle it with your favorite color of crayon.

add	poem
count	puzzle
match	read
measure	subtract
pattern	touch

Introduction to Strength

This section includes fitness and character development activities that focus on strength. These activities are designed to get your child moving and to get him thinking about strengthening his body and his character.

Physical Strength

Like flexibility, strength is an important component of good health. Many children may think that the only people who are strong are people who can lift an enormous amount of weight. However, strength is more than the ability to pick up heavy dumbbells. Explain that strength is built over time and point out to your child how much stronger he has become since he was a toddler.

Everyday activities and many fun exercises provide opportunities for children to gain strength. Your child could carry grocery bags to build his arms, ride a bicycle to develop his legs, or swim for a full-body strength workout. Classic exercises such as push-ups and chin-ups are also fantastic strength builders.

Help your child set realistic, achievable goals to improve his strength based on the activities that he enjoys. Over the summer months, offer encouragement and praise as your child gains strength and accomplishes his strength goals.

Strength of Character

As your child is building his physical strength, guide him to work on his inner strength as well. Explain that having strong character means standing up for his values, even if others do not agree with his viewpoint. Explain that it is not always easy to show inner strength. Discuss real-life examples, such as a time that he may have been teased by another child at the playground. How did he use his inner strength to handle the situation?

Remind your child that inner strength can be shown in many ways. For example, your child can show strength by being honest, by standing up for someone who needs his help, and by putting his best efforts into every task. Use your time together over the summer to help your child develop his strength, both physically and emotionally. Look for moments to acknowledge when he has demonstrated strength of character so that he can see the positive growth that he has achieved on the inside.

Add to find each sum. Place beans on the jar below to help you solve the problems.

1. 1	2. 2	3. 1	4. 3
+ 1	+ 2	+ 2	+ 1

5. 2	6. 3	7. 1	8. 2
+ 1	+ 2	+ 3	+ 3

Trace and color the picture.

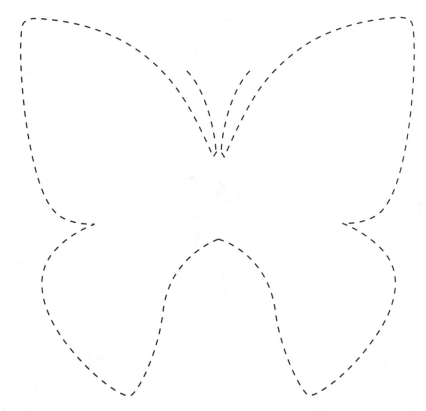

DAY 1

Yo-yo begins with the /y/ sound. Practice writing uppercase and lowercase **Y**s.

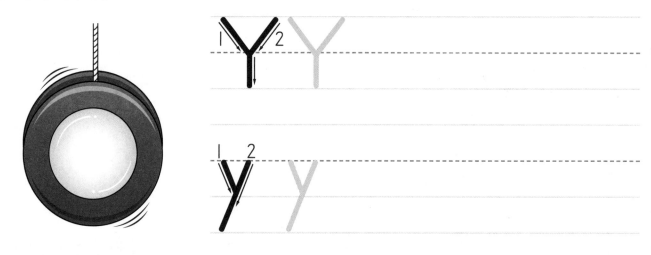

Say the name of each picture. Circle each picture that begins with the /y/ sound, like *yo-yo*.

Yogurt

FACTOID: The oldest yo-yo ever found is more than 2,000 years old.

PLACE STICKER HERE

Add to find each sum.

1.	5	
	+ 0	

2.	3	
	+ 3	

3.	1	
	+ 4	

4.	4	
	+ 2	

5.	2	
	+ 0	

1.   5   2.   3   3.   1   4.   4   5.   2
+ 0   + 3   + 4   + 2   + 0

6.   2   7.   4   8.   3   9.   5   10.   0
+ 3   + 0   + 4   + 1   + 3

Pull-Up Challenge

Visit a playground with an adult. Ask him to show you how to do a pull-up on a jungle gym bar. Try to do one pull-up. Hold on to the jungle gym bar and pull yourself up until your chin goes over the bar. It takes a lot of strength to complete one pull-up!

If you can, try to do more than one pull-up. If you have trouble with this exercise, ask the adult to help you complete a pull-up by holding your lower body as you pull up. Challenge yourself to practice this exercise regularly during the summer to see how many pull-ups you can complete. Have an adult help you set a summer pull-up goal.

* See page ii.

DAY 2

Zigzag begins with the /z/ sound. Practice writing uppercase and lowercase Zs.

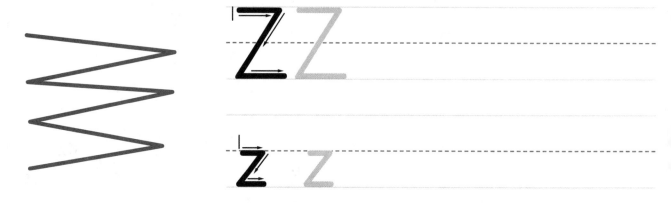

Say the name of each picture. Circle each picture that begins with the /z/ sound, like *zigzag*.

FITNESS FLASH: Do 10 lunges.

* See page ii.

PLACE STICKER HERE

Add to find each sum.

1. 3 + 1 = _____

2. 4 + 1 = _____

3. 3 + 0 = _____

4. 2 + 2 = _____

5. 1 + 3 = _____

6. 5 + 0 = _____

7. 1 + 4 = _____

8. 2 + 3 = _____

9. 1 + 1 = _____

Say the name of each shape. Use the key to color each shape.

◯ = red   ☐ = purple   △ = green   ▭ = blue

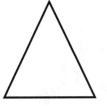
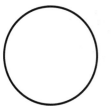

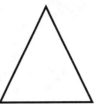
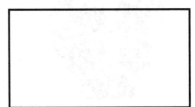

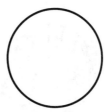

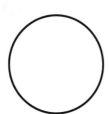

DAY 3

Ant begins with the short *a* sound. Practice writing uppercase and lowercase As.

Say the name of each picture. Circle each picture that has the short *a* sound, like *ant*.

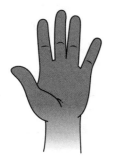  

FACTOID: An ant can lift 20 times its own weight.

PLACE
STICKER
HERE

Follow the directions to complete each problem.

1. Draw an X on the largest plate.

2. Circle the smallest spoon.

  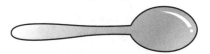

3. Circle the largest pie. Draw an X on the smallest pie.

Trace and write each letter.

DAY 4

Say the name of each picture. Write the missing short _a_.
EXAMPLE:

 a_nt

4.  f__n

5.  c__t

6.  m__p

7. v__n

8. c__p

Say each word. Listen for the short _a_ sound. Draw an X on the word that does not have the short _a_ sound.

man

ant	ran
sad	bed
bag	can
had	tag

FITNESS FLASH: Do five push-ups.

* See page ii.

58

PLACE STICKER HERE

Follow the directions to complete each problem.

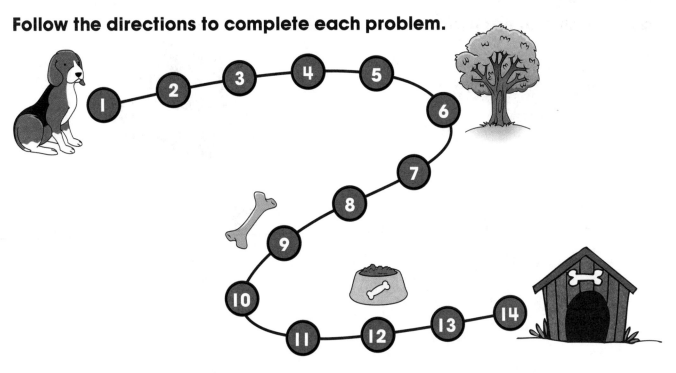

1. Fido takes 6 steps forward. What is he standing beside? _____

2. Then, Fido takes 1 step backward. He takes 4 steps forward. What

    does Fido find? _____

3. How many more steps must Fido take until he reaches his doghouse?

    _____

Honesty Journal

Being honest means being truthful. Make an honesty journal with an adult. Fold a sheet of construction paper to make the cover. Place blank paper inside the cover. Staple along the left side. Write the title, *A True Look at Honesty*, on the front cover. Use craft supplies to decorate the cover.

Draw pictures of yourself acting honestly. Show and explain what happens when you tell the truth and what happens when you do not tell the truth. Show your honesty journal to an adult. Talk about your drawings.

DAY 5

Say the name of each picture. Circle the name of each picture.

4.
rat
ran

5.
hat
has

6.
mat
map

7.
bag
bat

8.
cap
can

9.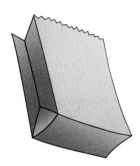
ball
bag

Read each sentence aloud. Listen for the short *a* sound. Circle each word that has the short *a* sound.

10. The cat ran and sat.

11. The sad rat jumped high.

12. Seth has a blue hat.

13. The man has two maps.

CHARACTER CHECK: Write five things that you are thankful for. Share your list with an adult.

PLACE STICKER HERE

Subtract to find each difference. Place beans on the jar below to help you solve the problems.

1. 2
    − 1

2. 3
    − 2

3. 4
    − 1

4. 5
    − 2

5. 3
    − 1

6. 2
    − 2

7. 4
    − 3

8. 5
    − 3

Trace each line. Color each section to make a rainbow.

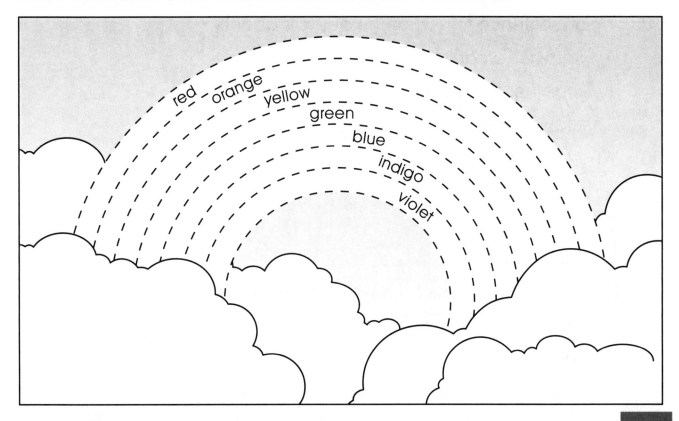

red   orange   yellow   green   blue   indigo   violet

DAY 6

Read the poem aloud. Listen for the short *a* sound. Draw a line under each word that has the short *a* sound.

Sam and Max

Sam has a cat.

Sam's cat is Max.

Max is a good cat.

Sam has a cap.

Max likes the cap.

Max sits on Sam's lap.

Sam has a bag.

Max runs to the bag.

Max naps on Sam's bag.

Read the poem again. Then, answer the questions.

9.   Which sentence tells what the poem is about?

   A.   Sam has a cat.

   B.   Max likes to wear a cap.

   C.   Max is a sleepy cat.

10.   Where did Max nap?

   A.   on the bed

   B.   on Sam's bag

   C.   on a mat

11.   How do you think Max feels when he sits on Sam's lap?

   A.   happy

   B.   sad

   C.   scared

FACTOID: The longest whiskers ever measured on a cat were 7.5 inches (19 cm) long.

Subtract to find each difference.

1. 5
   – 1

2. 6
   – 2

3. 6
   – 3

4. 5
   – 5

5. 5
   – 4

6. 4
   – 2

7. 2
   – 1

8. 3
   – 3

9. 6
   – 1

10. 3
    – 0

Complete each pattern.

11.   _____ _____

12.   _____ _____

13.   _____ _____

DAY 7

Egg begins with the short *e* sound. Practice writing uppercase and lowercase **E**s.

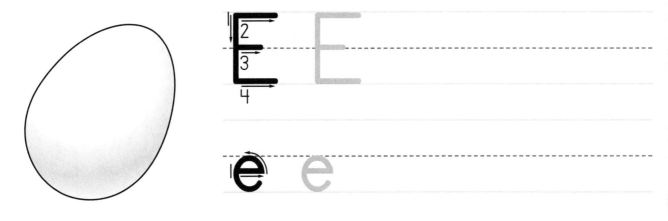

Say the name of each picture. Circle each picture that has the short *e* sound, like *egg*.

FITNESS FLASH: Do 10 squats.

* See page ii.

PLACE STICKER HERE

Subtract to find each difference.

1. 3 – 1 = _____

2. 3 – 2 = _____

3. 4 – 2 = _____

4. 4 – 1 = _____

5. 5 – 4 = _____

6. 5 – 3 = _____

7. 2 – 1 = _____

8. 4 – 3 = _____

9. 4 – 0 = _____

Trace and write each letter.

DAY 8

Say the name of each picture. Write the missing short *e*.
EXAMPLE:

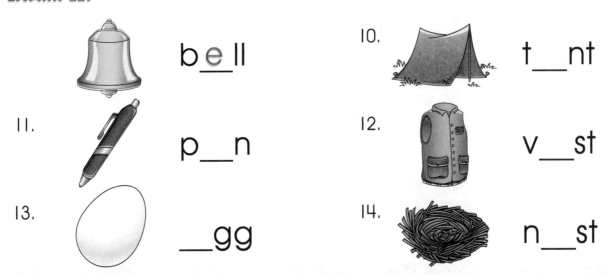

b_e_ll

10. t__nt

11. p__n

12. v__st

13. __gg

14. n__st

Say each word. Listen for the short *e* sound. Draw an X on the word that does not have the short *e* sound.

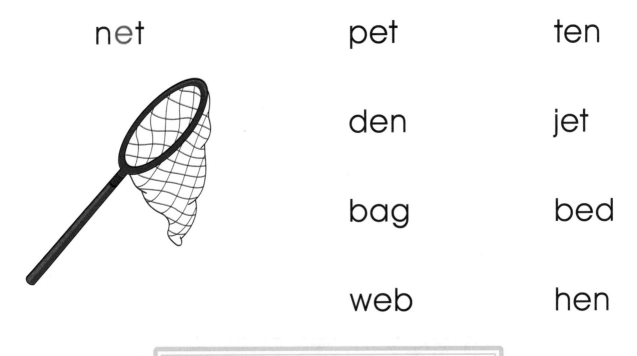

net

pet   ten

den   jet

bag   bed

web   hen

FACTOID: Lions live in groups called *prides.*

PLACE
STICKER
HERE

Subtract to find each difference.

1.   7
    − 3

2.   6
    − 5

3.   9
    − 4

4.   6
    − 4

5.   9
    − 8

6.   8
    − 8

7.   8
    − 5

8.   5
    − 5

9.   6
    − 2

10.   7
    − 6

Complete the second picture to match the first picture in each set.

11.
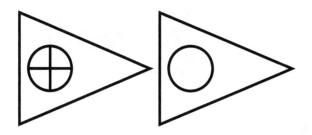

12.
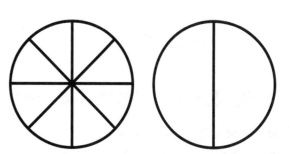

13.

14.
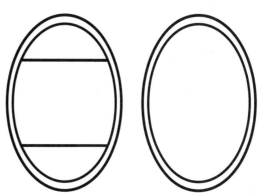

DAY 9

Say the name of each picture. Circle the name of each picture.

15.
web
wet

16.
nest
net

17.
let
jet

18.
ten
hen

19.
belt
bell

20.
bed
best

Read each sentence aloud. Listen for the short *e* sound. Circle each word that has the short *e* sound.

21. Jed is in his bed.

22. Peg has a pet hen.

23. Ben and Wes have five toy jets.

24. Beth has a red pen.

 FITNESS FLASH: Do 10 sit-ups.

* See page ii.

 PLACE STICKER HERE

Circle the numbers that match the first number in each row.

12	21	12	15	12	51	12	21	12
96	96	99	66	86	96	66	96	96
54	55	54	45	43	54	45	54	52
71	71	17	71	11	71	71	17	71
35	53	55	35	35	33	35	53	35

Color each crayon to match the color word.

 red   blue

 yellow   green

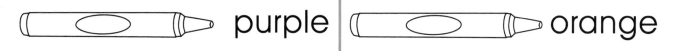 purple   orange

 brown   black

DAY 10

Read the poem aloud. Listen for the short _e_ sound. Draw a line under each word that has the short _e_ sound.

Meg the Vet

Meg is a vet.

Vets help sick pets.

Vets help pets get well.

Some vets help big pets.

Some vets help small pets.

Vets can wrap a dog's leg.

Vets can mend a horse's head.

Vets can fix a cat with no pep.

Vets can also help your pet.

Meg likes being a vet.

Read the poem again. Then, answer the questions.

1. Which sentence tells what the poem is about?

   A. Pets get sick.

   B. Vets help sick pets.

   C. Cats have no pep.

2. Whom do vets help? _____

3. Write _T_ for things that are true. Write _F_ for things that are false.

   _____ Meg likes being a vet.

   _____ Vets help small pets.

   _____ Vets fix cars.

CHARACTER CHECK: Write a song about respecting all of Earth's creatures. Share your song with an adult.

PLACE STICKER HERE

A ruler is used to measure length. This ruler measures in inches. Use a ruler to measure the length of each line to the nearest inch.

1. _____ _____ inches

2. _____ _____ inches

3. _____ _____ inches

4. _____ _____ inches

Practice writing your name on the lines. The three lines are different sizes.

DAY 11

Iguana begins with the short *i* sound. Practice writing uppercase and lowercase Is.

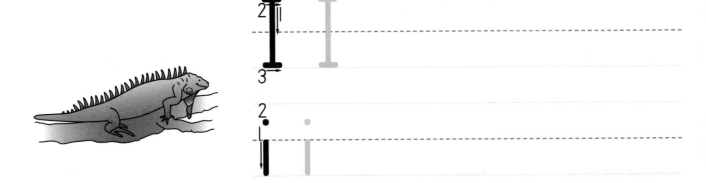

Say the name of each picture. Circle each picture that has the short *i* sound, like *iguana*.

FACTOID: Safety pins have been used for more than 2,500 years.

© Carson-Dellosa

A ruler is used to measure length. This ruler measures in centimeters. Use a ruler to measure the length of each line to the nearest centimeter.

1. ━━━━━━━━━━━━━━━━━━━━━━━━━ _____ centimeters

2. ━━━━━━━━━━━━━━━━ _____ centimeters

3.  _____ centimeters

4.  _____ centimeters

Draw a line to match each number to the set with the same number of objects.

1

2

3

4

5

Say the name of each picture. Write the missing short _i_.
EXAMPLE:

w_i_g

5.
s__nk

6.
m__lk

7.
b__b

8.
sh__p

9.
s__x

Say each word. Listen for the short _i_ sound. Draw an X on the word that does not have the short _i_ sound.

pin   did   hid

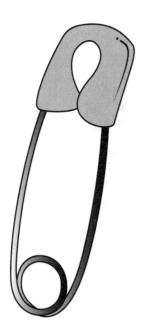   bug   win

               in   it

               sit   is

 FITNESS FLASH: Do 10 lunges.

* See page ii.

Circle the largest object in each group.

1.
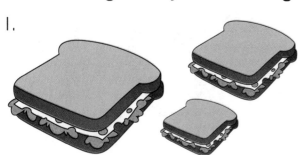

2.

Circle the smallest object in each group.

3.

4.
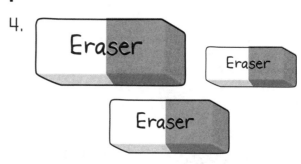

Circle the picture that matches the first picture in each row.

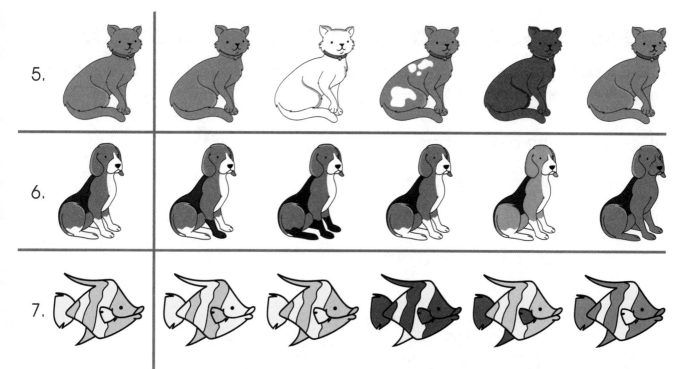

5.

6.

7.

DAY 13

Say the name of each picture. Circle the name of each picture.

8.
fish

wish

9.
rug

ring

10.
pit

pin

11.
sit

six

12.
win

wig

13.
lips

leg

Read each sentence aloud. Listen for the short _i_ sound. Circle each word that has the short _i_ sound.

14. Jim hid the bib in a bag.

15. The fish swim in the pond.

16. The big cat did a flip.

17. Jill will teach the boy to swim.

FACTOID: Swimming has been an Olympic sport in all of the modern Olympic Games.

PLACE STICKER HERE

Count the frogs in the pond. Answer the questions.

1. How many frogs are in the pond?

   _____

2. How many frogs will be in the pond if 3 frogs hop away?

   _____

Draw a line to match each number to the set with the same number of objects.

6

7

8

9

10

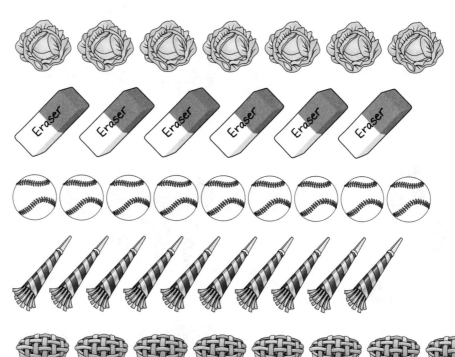

DAY 14

Ostrich begins with the short *o* sound. Practice writing uppercase and lowercase Os.

Say the name of each picture. Circle each picture that has the short *o* sound, like *ostrich*.

FITNESS FLASH: Do five push-ups.

* See page ii.

PLACE STICKER HERE

Look at the picture. Read each question. Circle the correct answer.

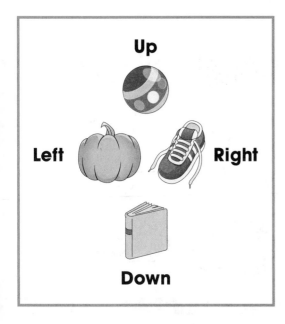

1. What is up?

2. What is down?

3. What is left?

4. What is right?

Write the name of each picture to solve the crossword puzzles.

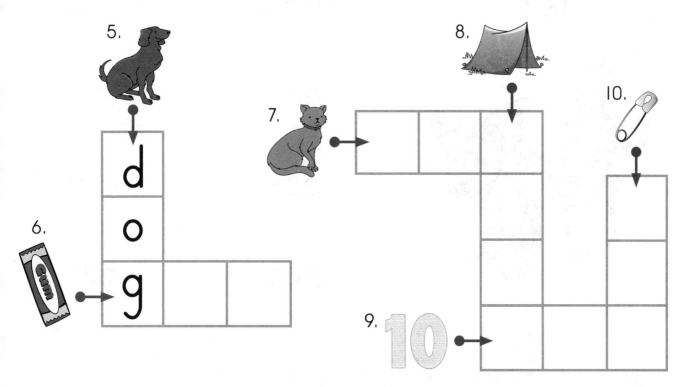

5. d o g

6.

7.

8.

9. 10

10.

DAY 15

Say the name of each object. Write the missing short _o_.
EXAMPLE:

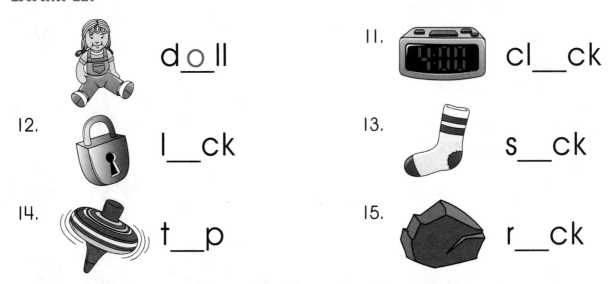

d_o_ll

11. cl__ck

12. l__ck

13. s__ck

14. t__p

15. r__ck

Say each word. Listen for the short _o_ sound. Draw an X on the word that does not have the short _o_ sound.

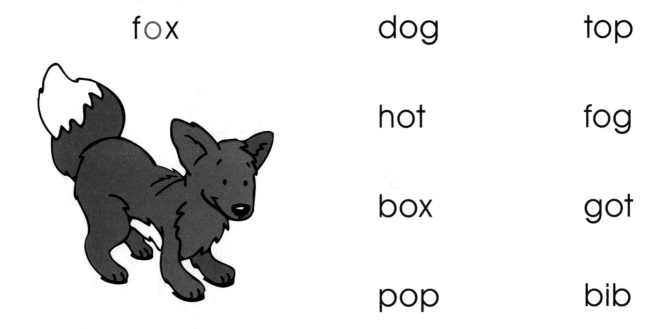

fox	dog	top
	hot	fog
	box	got
	pop	bib

CHARACTER CHECK: What does it mean to be brave? Look up the word in a dictionary with an adult.

PLACE STICKER HERE

Circle the object in each group that holds more.

1.

2.

Circle the object in each group that holds less.

3.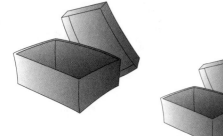

4.

Draw a line to match each opposite.

up

 day

night

 sad

 happy

 down

DAY 16

Say the name of each picture. Circle the name of each picture.

5.

jog
job

6.

doll
dog

7.

bag
box

8.

mop
mat

9.

fox
box

10.

frog
foot

Read each sentence aloud. Listen for the short *o* sound. Circle each word that has the short *o* sound.

11. The frog can hop on top of the box.

12. The dog and the fox ran to the pond.

13. John put the box by the rock.

14. Tom went for a jog.

FACTOID: The smallest species of frog is less than one inch long when fully grown.

PLACE STICKER HERE

Follow the directions to color the gumballs.

Color 1 gumball red.

Color 1 gumball orange.

Color 3 gumballs yellow.

Color 2 gumballs green.

Color 3 gumballs blue.

Color 2 gumballs purple.

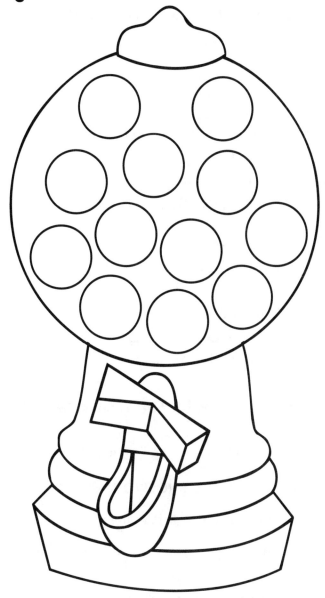

Arm Curls

Collect empty water bottles of different sizes. Hold an empty water bottle in each hand and do arm curls. Fill the bottles with water. Make sure that the lids are on tight! Try to do arm curls with the full bottles. Which bottles take more strength to lift, the larger or smaller bottles? How many arm curls can you do with each arm?

* See page ii.

DAY 17

Read the poem aloud. Listen for the short *o* sound. Draw a line under each word that has the short *o* sound.

Rob the Dog

A frog sat on a log by the pond.
Along came a dog named Rob.
Rob, the dog, sat on the log.
The dog sang a song.
The frog did not like the song.
The frog hopped off the log.

Along came a fox.
The fox sat on the log.
Rob, the dog, sat on the log.
The dog sang a song.
The fox did not like the song.
The fox popped off the log.

Read the poem again. Then, answer the questions.

1. Which animal sang the song? _____

2. Why did the frog leave the log?

   A. The fox sat on the log. B. The dog sat on the log.

   C. The frog did not like the song. D. The frog wanted to sing.

3. How did the frog leave the log? _____

4. How did the fox leave the log? _____

5. Write another good title for the poem. _____

FITNESS FLASH: Do 10 squats.

* See page ii.

PLACE STICKER HERE

Circle the word that completes each sentence.

1.

The fish is _____ the bowl.

      in   out

2.

The bird is _____ the cloud.

      over   under

Read each short vowel word in the word bank. Find and circle each word in the puzzle. Words can be found across and down.

hen	men	pin
sad	sun	up

```
w  p  i  n  u
s  a  d  l  o
l  f  s  u  n
h  e  n  p  m
t  m  e  n  b
```

DAY 18

Umbrella begins with the short *u* sound. Practice writing uppercase and lowercase Us.

Say the name of each picture. Circle each picture that has the short *u* sound, like *umbrella*.

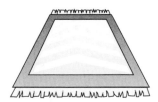

FACTOID: *Parasol* is another word for *umbrella.*

PLACE STICKER HERE

Touch each number in order. Say it aloud with an adult.

1	2	3	4	5	6	7	8	9	10
11	12	13	14	15	16	17	18	19	20
21	22	23	24	25	26	27	28	29	30
31	32	33	34	35	36	37	38	39	40
41	42	43	44	45	46	47	48	49	50
51	52	53	54	55	56	57	58	59	60
61	62	63	64	65	66	67	68	69	70
71	72	73	74	75	76	77	78	79	80
81	82	83	84	85	86	87	88	89	90
91	92	93	94	95	96	97	98	99	100

DAY 19

Say the name of each picture. Write the missing short _u_.
EXAMPLE:

 h _u_ g

1. r ___ g

2. d ___ ck

3. s ___ n

4.  t ___ b

5. m ___ g

Say each word. Listen for the short _u_ sound. Draw an X on the word that does not have the short _u_ sound.

gum

mud   fun

dug   hat

cut   us

up   hut

FITNESS FLASH: Do 10 sit-ups.

* See page ii.

PLACE STICKER HERE

On each number line, draw a dot on the first even number. Then, skip count by 2s. Draw a dot on each even number in the pattern. The first pattern has been started for you.

1.

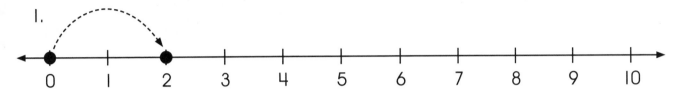

2.

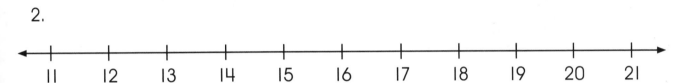

Use the calendar to answer each question.

July

Sunday	Monday	Tuesday	Wednesday	Thursday	Friday	Saturday
		1	2	3	4	5
6	7	8	9	10	11	12
13	14	15	16	17	18	19
20	21	22	23	24	25	26
27	28	29	30	31		

3. What day of the week is

    July 23? _____

4. What day of the week is the

    last day of July? _____

5. What date is the second

    Tuesday? _____

6. What day of the week is

    July 4? _____

Say the name of each picture. Circle the name of each picture.

7.
sun
sub

8.
gum
gem

9.
bud
bus

10.
rug
rag

11.
duck
dock

12.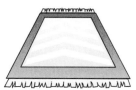
net
nut

Read each sentence aloud. Listen for the short _u_ sound. Circle each word that has the short _u_ sound.

13. The lucky duck swam on the pond.

14. Mom cut the bud off of the bush.

15. Gus chewed gum on the bus.

16. Judd washed the mud out of the rug.

CHARACTER CHECK: Why should you always tell the truth?

Constellations

A constellation is a group of stars that make a pattern. How can you make a constellation in your room?

Materials:
- flashlight
- round cardboard container
- sharpened pencil

Procedure:
Look at the night sky with an adult to see the different constellations. Choose a constellation that you would like to create or create your own star pattern. Have an adult use the pencil to punch holes in the

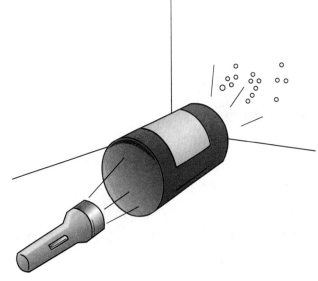

bottom of the round cardboard container. Then, turn out the lights. Shine the flashlight into the open end of the cardboard container to make the star pattern appear on your ceiling or wall.

1. Which constellation did you create? If you created your own

   constellation, name it. _____

2. When can you see stars in the sky? _____

3. What else can you see in the night sky? _____

   _____

Grasping Objects

How do your thumbs help you grasp objects?

Materials:
- tape
- pencil
- several small objects

Procedure:

Have an adult help you tape the thumb of your writing hand to your palm so that you cannot move it. The tape should allow your other fingers to move freely. Try to pick up a pencil and write your name. Then, try to tie your shoes. Next, try to pick up each small object.

Remove the tape. Repeat each activity. Notice how your thumb works as you complete each activity.

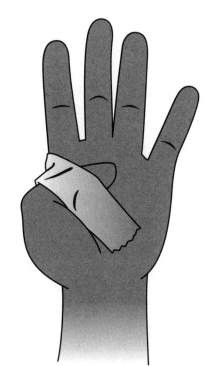

1. Circle the activity that was easier.

    A. writing with a taped hand

    B. writing with no tape on your hand

2. Circle the activity that was more difficult.

    A. tying your shoe with no tape on your hand

    B. tying your shoe with a taped hand

3. Circle the names of the animals who have thumbs that help them grasp objects.

    monkey   fish

    frog   gorilla

It's Only Natural!

Look at each object. Write _M_ if the object is made by people. Write _N_ if the object is natural (not made by people).

1.  _____

2.  _____

3.  _____

4.  _____

5.  _____

6.  _____

7.  _____

8.  _____

9.  _____

10.  _____

BONUS

Globe

Color the water blue. Color the land green. Have an adult help you find a map or a globe online or at a library to check your coloring.

Travel Today

Look at the wagon. In the past, people used horse-drawn wagons to travel long distances. Draw what we use to travel today.

PAST

PRESENT

BONUS

Take It Outside!

Go outside with an adult. Choose an object and place it on a hard surface. Use a piece of chalk to trace the outline of the object's shadow. Return to the object at a different time of day and trace the shadow again. What do you notice about the two shadows?

Go outside with an adult. Look for different places where animals make their homes, such as in trees or creeks. Make sure not to touch any animals or their homes! What kind of animal do you think lives in each home?

Go outside with an adult. Collect five leaves. Talk about the leaves with the adult. Are they the same color? Are they the same shape? Did they fall from trees or bushes? How are they alike, and how are they different?

* See page ii.

Monthly Goals

Think of three goals that you would like to set for yourself this month. For example, you may want to learn three new words each week. Have an adult help you write your goals on the lines.

Place a sticker next to each goal that you complete. Feel proud that you have met your goals!

1. _____ PLACE STICKER HERE

2. _____ PLACE STICKER HERE

3. _____ PLACE STICKER HERE

Word List

The following words are used in this section. They are good words for you to know. Read each word aloud with an adult. When you see a word from this list on a page, circle it with your favorite color of crayon.

answer	pretend
clock	real
family	rhyme
half	spell
money	time

Introduction to Endurance

This section includes fitness and character development activities that focus on endurance. These activities are designed to get your child moving and to get her thinking about developing her physical and mental stamina.

Physical Endurance

Many children seem to have endless energy and can run, jump, and play for hours. But, other children may not have developed that kind of endurance. Improving endurance requires regular aerobic exercise, which causes the heart to beat faster and the person to breathe harder. As a result of regular aerobic activity, the heart becomes stronger, and the blood cells deliver oxygen to the body more efficiently. There are many ways for a child to get an aerobic workout that does not feel like exercise. Jumping rope and playing tag are examples.

Summer provides a variety of opportunities to bolster your child's endurance. If you see your child head for the TV, suggest an activity that will get her moving instead. Explain that while there are times when a relaxing indoor activity is valuable, it is important to take advantage of the warm mornings and sunny days to go outdoors. Reserve the less active times for when it is dark, too hot, or raining. Explain the importance of physical activity and invite her to join you for a walk, a bike ride, or a game of basketball.

Endurance and Character Development

Endurance applies to the mind as well as to the body. Explain to your child that *endurance* means to stick with something. Children can demonstrate mental endurance every day. For example, staying with a task when she might want to quit and keeping at it until it is done are ways that a child can show endurance.

Take advantage of summertime to help your child practice her mental endurance. Look for situations where she might seem frustrated or bored. Perhaps she asked to take swimming lessons, but after a few early-morning classes, she is not having as much fun as she had imagined. Turn this dilemma into a learning opportunity. It is important that children feel some ownership in decision making, so guide her to some key points to consider, such as how she asked all spring for permission to take lessons. Remind her that she has taken only a few lessons, so she might get used to the early-morning practices. Let her know that she has options to make the experience more enjoyable, such as going to bed earlier or sleeping a few extra minutes during the morning ride to lessons. Explain that quitting should be the last resort. Teaching your child at a young age to endure will help her as she continues to develop into a happy, healthy person.

Add or subtract to solve each problem.

1. 2
  + 3

2. 1
  + 4

3. 5
  + 2

4. 3
  + 0

5. 3
  + 4

6. 2
  - 1

7. 8
  - 6

8. 9
  - 5

9. 4
  - 3

10. 4
   - 1

Write the missing numbers.

1	2								
					16				
		23							
								39	
			44						50

DAY 1

Read the passage. Answer the questions.

Pups and Cubs

Pups and cubs are little and cute. Pups make good pets. Cubs do not.

Pups are baby dogs. They like to run. Cubs are baby bears. They like to run too. You can run with pups but not with cubs. A pup's mother would be glad if you ran with her pup. But, a cub's mother would be mad if you ran with her cub.

Pups and cubs like to tug. Pups are fun to play tug with, but a cub's tug can be too much! So, pick a pup for a pet, not a cub.

11. Which sentence tells what the passage is about?

    A. Cubs like to run.

    B. Pups make good pets, but cubs do not.

    C. Pups and cubs are cute.

12. What is a pup?

    A. a mother bear

    B. a baby bear

    C. a baby dog

13. Write four short *u* words from the passage.

_____ _____ _____ _____

FACTOID: There are eight species of bears in the world.

PLACE STICKER HERE

When you count pennies, you count by 1s. Count each set of pennies. Write the total amount.

1.

_____ ¢

2.

_____ ¢

3.

_____ ¢

4.

_____ ¢

Write the missing numbers.

51	52								
				65					
		73							
						87			
			94						100

DAY 2

Say the name of each picture. Circle the pictures with the same beginning sound as the letter in each row.

5.

f

6.

c

7.

d

8.

g

9.

h

FITNESS FLASH: Do 10 jumping jacks.

* See page ii.

PLACE STICKER HERE

Count by 2s. Write the missing numbers on the train cars.

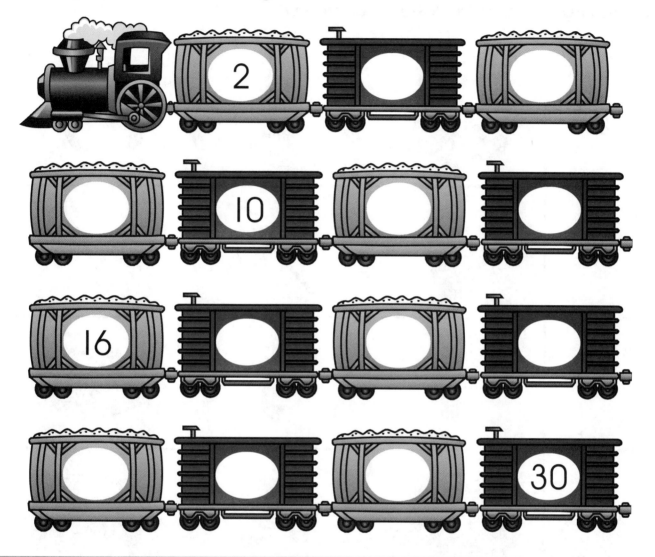

Obstacle Course

Having endurance means that you can exercise harder and for longer amounts of time. The more you exercise, the easier it will be each time. Use this activity to improve your endurance.

Create an obstacle course with an adult. Use soft objects from around your home to create obstacles to run around, jump over, crawl through, or carry. As you build endurance, add new obstacles to the course. How many times in a row can you complete the obstacle course?

* See page ii.

DAY 3

Say the name of each picture. Circle the pictures with the same beginning sound as the letter in each row.

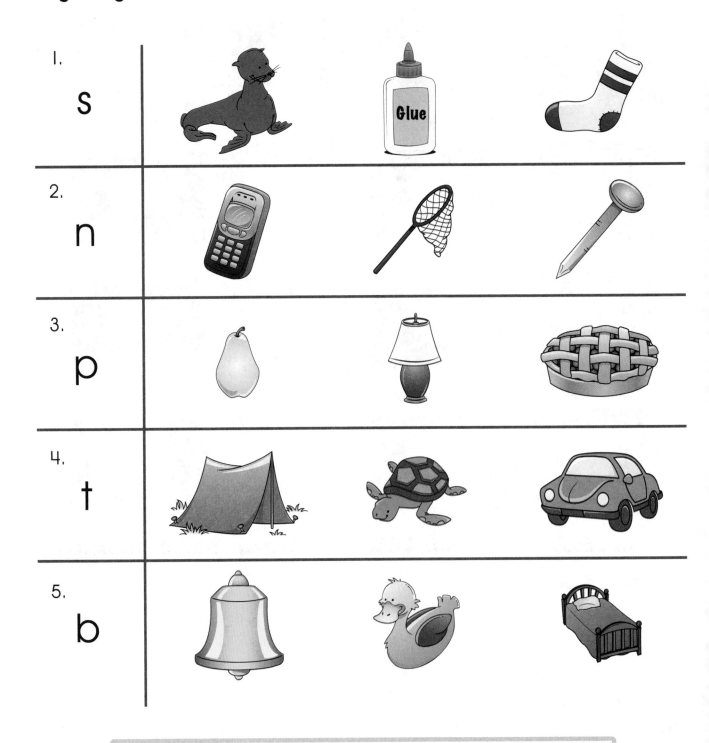

1. s

2. n

3. p

4. t

5. b

FACTOID: A human blinks about 17,280 times a day on average.

PLACE STICKER HERE

Count by 5s. Write the numbers on the lines.

_____ _____ _____ _____ _____

_____ _____ _____ _____ _____

Think of a special holiday, custom, or tradition that your family observes. Draw and color a picture of your family and the holiday. Write each person's name beside his or her picture.

DAY 4

Say the name of each picture. Circle the pictures with the same beginning sound as the letter in each row.

1. **j**	baseball	jar	jet
2. **r**	rabbit	horse	ring
3. **k**	key	hat	kite
4. **w**	web	apple	watch
5. **z**	zebra	zipper	tent

FITNESS FLASH: Jog in place for 30 seconds.

* See page ii.

PLACE STICKER HERE

DAY 5

When you count nickels, you count by 5s. Count each set of nickels. Write the total amount.

1.

_____ ¢

2.

_____ ¢

3.

_____ ¢

4.

_____ ¢

Read each word. Circle the pictures in each row that rhyme with the word.

5. cat

6. fan

7. hop

DAY 5

Read the story. Answer the questions.

Tasha the Zookeeper

Tasha is a zookeeper. Her job is to keep the animals safe and happy. She cleans the habitats and gives the animals food and water.

Last week, a hawk began to squawk. Tasha saw that he had a hurt wing. She called a vet to fix the hawk's wing. Later, she helped a lion with a sore paw. Soon, the lion was strong and **healthy**. Then, Tasha cleaned the bears' home. She hid a treat for the bears to find. Tasha enjoys her job.

8. Which sentence tells what the story is about?

   A. Tasha takes care of the animals at the zoo.

   B. Tasha is safe and happy.

   C. The animals like Tasha.

9. What happened to the hawk?

   A. The hawk could not sing.

   B. The hawk had a hurt wing.

   C. The hawk was hungry.

10. What does *healthy* mean?

   A. sick

   B. well

   C. weak

11. What does Tasha do at her job? _____

_____

_____

CHARACTER CHECK: Think of a time when you helped a friend or family member. How did helping make you feel? Draw a picture of how you helped.

PLACE
STICKER
HERE

Count by 10s. Write the missing numbers.

10			40	50
60		80		100

Draw a house to match the first house. Color the houses.

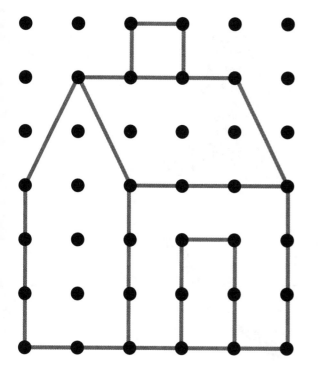

DAY 6

Say the name of each picture. Write the letter of the beginning sound.
EXAMPLE:

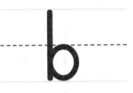

b

1.

_____

2.

- - - - - - - - -

3.

- - - - - - - - -

4.

- - - - - - - - -

5.

- - - - - - - - -

6.

- - - - - - - - -

7.

- - - - - - - - -

FACTOID: Australia's Great Barrier Reef can be seen from outer space.

PLACE
STICKER
HERE

When you count dimes, you count by 10s. Count each set of dimes. Write the total amount.

1.

_____ ¢

2.

_____ ¢

3.

_____ ¢

4.

_____ ¢

How many ways can you think of to make 25¢ using only pennies, nickels, and dimes? Draw coins in the space below. Use real money if you need help.

EXAMPLE: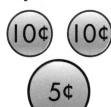

DAY 7

Say the name of each picture. Write the letter of the beginning sound.
EXAMPLE:

m

5.

_____

6.

_____

7.

_____

8.

_____

9.

_____

10.

_____

11.

_____

FITNESS FLASH: Hop on your right foot for 30 seconds.

* See page ii.

PLACE
STICKER
HERE

Add to find each sum.

1.	5	2.	4	3.	9	4.	2	5.	3	6.	8
	+ 3		+ 5		+ 1		+ 7		+ 4		+ 2

7.	9	8.	1	9.	5	10.	5	11.	6	12.	3
	+ 0		+ 8		+ 5		+ 2		+ 2		+ 5

Connect the dots from A to Z. Start at the ★. Color the picture.

DAY 8

Read the poem. Answer the questions.

Our Tree House

My friend and I are way up high
watching as the world goes by
in our tree house.

Down on the ground
little people move around
below our tree house.

Birds fly above and below us.
They **screech** and make a loud fuss
around our tree house.

13. Who is in the tree house?

    A. two monkeys

    B. two friends

    C. two dogs

14. What does *screech* mean?

    A. to circle

    B. to make a loud sound

    C. to stand

15. Write four words from the poem that rhyme with *my*.

16. Write another good title for the poem.

FACTOID: One of the largest wooden tree houses
in the world has a restaurant and a gift shop inside it.

PLACE
STICKER
HERE

Add to find each sum.

1. 6 + 2 = _____   2. 5 + 1 = _____   3. 4 + 3 = _____

4. 1 + 7 = _____   5. 2 + 8 = _____   6. 9 + 0 = _____

7. 3 + 5 = _____   8. 4 + 6 = _____   9. 7 + 2 = _____

10. 8 + 1 = _____   11. 1 + 9 = _____   12. 6 + 3 = _____

Read each number word in the word bank. Find and circle each word in the puzzle. Words can be found across and down.

| one | two | three | four | five | six | seven | eight | nine | ten |

```
m  a  z  t  s  i  x
t  e  n  w  x  o  p
y  i  f  o  u  r  o
f  g  s  e  v  e  n
i  h  l  n  i  n  e
v  t  h  r  e  e  b
e  c  d  e  f  g  h
```

DAY 9

Say the name of each picture. Circle the letter of the ending sound.
EXAMPLE:

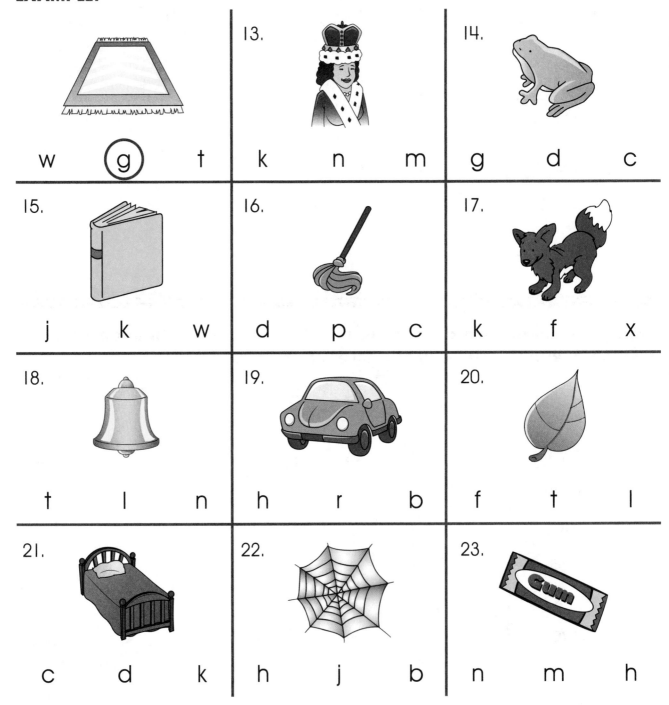

w (g) t	13. k n m	14. g d c
15. j k w	16. d p c	17. k f x
18. t l n	19. h r b	20. f t l
21. c d k	22. h j b	23. n m h

FITNESS FLASH: Hop on your left foot 10 times.

* See page ii.

PLACE
STICKER
HERE

Subtract to find each difference.

1.	7	2.	8	3.	9	4.	6	5.	5	6.	8
	− 3		− 5		− 1		− 2		− 4		− 3

7.	6	8.	8	9.	5	10.	7	11.	9	12.	8
	− 3		− 7		− 2		− 5		− 4		− 6

Draw and color a picture of something that is real.	**Draw and color a picture of something that is pretend.**

DAY 10

Say the name of each picture. Write the letter of the ending sound.
EXAMPLE:

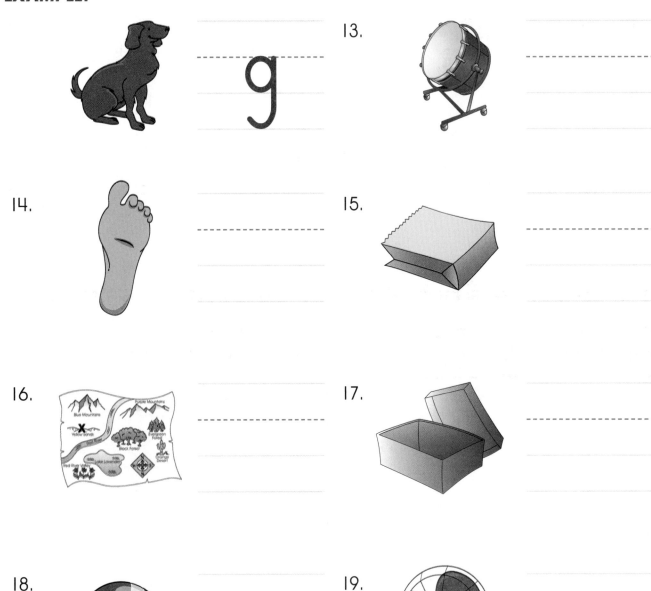

g

13.

14.

15.

16.

17.

18.

19.

CHARACTER CHECK: Make a card for a friend or family member that you have not seen in a long time. Ask an adult to help you mail your card.

PLACE STICKER HERE

Subtract to find each difference.

1. 5 – 2 = _____

2. 9 – 3 = _____

3. 10 – 1 = _____

4. 7 – 4 = _____

5. 6 – 2 = _____

6. 8 – 5 = _____

7. 9 – 5 = _____

8. 10 – 2 = _____

9. 7 – 3 = _____

10. 8 – 4 = _____

11. 5 – 5 = _____

12. 6 – 3 = _____

13. 10 – 0 = _____

14. 6 – 4 = _____

15. 5 – 3 = _____

Draw lines to match the pictures whose names rhyme.

DAY 11

Say the name of each picture. Write the letters of the beginning and ending sounds.

EXAMPLE:

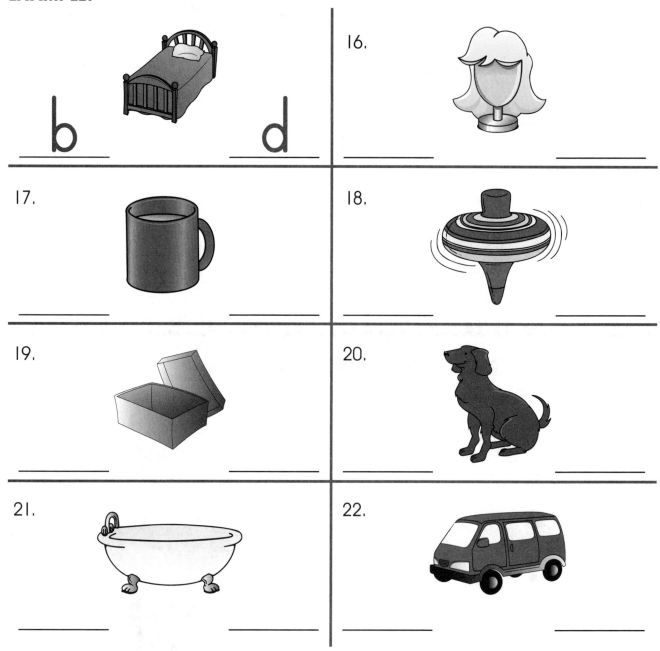

b ___ ___ d

16. ___ ___

17. ___ ___

18. ___ ___

19. ___ ___

20. ___ ___

21. ___ ___

22. ___ ___

FACTOID: The average worker honeybee produces one-twelfth of a teaspoon of honey in its lifetime.

PLACE STICKER HERE

Add or subtract to solve each problem.

1. 　7
　 + 3

2. 　8
　 − 2

3. 　9
　 − 5

4. 　6
　 + 2

5. 　5
　 + 3

6. 　1
　 + 8

7. 　6
　 − 3

8. 　8
　 − 7

9. 　9
　 + 1

10. 　7
　 − 5

11. 　9
　 − 4

12. 　8
　 − 6

Circle the two pictures in each row with names that rhyme.

13.

14.

15.

DAY 12

Read the story. Answer the questions.

Andre's Birthday

Andre's birthday was on Saturday. He had a very busy day.

In the morning, he went to breakfast with his grandmother. He had pancakes and juice. He ate all of the pancakes.

Then, Andre and six friends saw a movie. After the movie, they went back to Andre's house. They played tag and hide-and-seek.

Andre's dad fixed Andre his favorite meal for dinner. He made grilled cheese sandwiches and fruit salad. He also baked a cake with white icing. It was good!

16. On what day was Andre's birthday?

   A. Wednesday

   B. Friday

   C. Saturday

17. Whom did Andre go to breakfast with?

   A. his dad

   B. his grandmother

   C. his friends

18. What did Andre have for breakfast?_____

_____

19. What did Andre and his friends do at Andre's house? _____

_____

FITNESS FLASH: Hop on your right foot for 30 seconds.

* See page ii.

PLACE STICKER HERE

Add or subtract to solve each problem.

1. $\begin{array}{r} 1 \\ + 1 \\ \hline \end{array}$ 2. $\begin{array}{r} 2 \\ + 2 \\ \hline \end{array}$ 3. $\begin{array}{r} 3 \\ + 3 \\ \hline \end{array}$ 4. $\begin{array}{r} 4 \\ + 4 \\ \hline \end{array}$ 5. $\begin{array}{r} 5 \\ + 5 \\ \hline \end{array}$ 6. $\begin{array}{r} 0 \\ + 0 \\ \hline \end{array}$

7. $\begin{array}{r} 1 \\ - 1 \\ \hline \end{array}$ 8. $\begin{array}{r} 2 \\ - 2 \\ \hline \end{array}$ 9. $\begin{array}{r} 3 \\ - 3 \\ \hline \end{array}$ 10. $\begin{array}{r} 4 \\ - 4 \\ \hline \end{array}$ 11. $\begin{array}{r} 5 \\ - 5 \\ \hline \end{array}$ 12. $\begin{array}{r} 0 \\ - 0 \\ \hline \end{array}$

Draw the other half of each picture. Color the pictures.

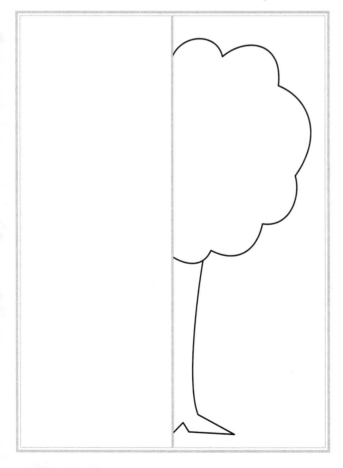
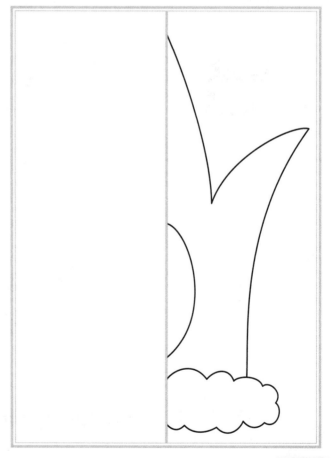

DAY 13

Say each word. Listen for the long *a* sound. Draw Xs on the two words that do not have the long *a* sound.

bake	cane	cage	tape
cake	lane	page	cape
tire	gate	rain	mane
ape	boat	pail	rake

Say the name of each picture. Write the letters you hear to spell each word.

13.

__ __ __ e

14.

__ __ __ e

15.

__ __ __ e

16.

__ __ i __

17.

__ __ i __

18.

__ __ i __ __

FACTOID: The first Olympic Games were held in July 776 BC in Greece.

PLACE STICKER HERE

Add or subtract to solve each problem.

1. $9 - 3 =$ _____

2. $6 + 4 =$ _____

3. $5 + 3 =$ _____

4. $2 + 7 =$ _____

5. $8 - 2 =$ _____

6. $7 - 5 =$ _____

7. $4 + 5 =$ _____

8. $6 - 3 =$ _____

9. $6 + 3 =$ _____

10. $8 - 3 =$ _____

11. $9 - 4 =$ _____

12. $9 - 5 =$ _____

13. $5 + 4 =$ _____

14. $4 - 3 =$ _____

15. $7 + 2 =$ _____

Write a number sentence to solve each problem.

16.

Three balloons float in the air. One balloon pops. How many balloons are left?

_____ − _____ = _____

17.

Five bees sat on a flower. Three bees flew away. How many bees are left?

_____ − _____ = _____

DAY 14

Say each word. Listen for the long e sound. Draw Xs on the two words that do not have the long e sound.

eel	queen	feet	rose
feel	seed	sweet	beak
pea	bead	rake	beach
meal	bean	jeans	steam

Say the name of each picture. Write the letters you hear to spell each word.

18.

__ __ __ __

19.

__ __ __ e

20.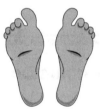

__ __ __ __

21.

__ __ a __ __

22.

__ __ a __

23.

__ __ a __

FITNESS FLASH: Do 10 jumping jacks.

* See page ii.

PLACE STICKER HERE

Count each set of blocks. Write the number.

1.

_____

2.
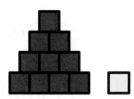

_____

3.
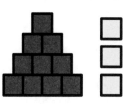

_____

4.
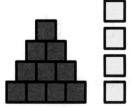

_____

5.
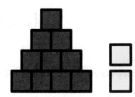

_____

6.
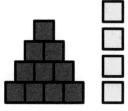

_____

Perseverance Payoff

Perseverance means trying even if something is difficult to do. Have an adult help you write a list of situations in which you can show perseverance, such as learning a new math skill.

Make a second list. Have an adult help you write ways to help you persevere through each situation. Make a third list that describes the rewards of persevering.

Remember that it is not always easy to persevere, but when you do, you will feel proud and happy about what you accomplished. When things get tough, do not give up. Imagine the benefits of always trying to do your best.

DAY 15

Say each word. Listen for the long *i* sound. Draw Xs on the two words that do not have the long *i* sound.

pie	wide	ripe	like
tie	side	pipe	hike
life	cute	rise	mile
wife	tire	wise	seed

Say the name of each picture. Write the letters you hear to spell each word.

7.
__ __ __ e

8.
__ __ e

9.
__ __ __ e

10.
__ __ __ e

11.
__ __ __ e

12.
__ __ __ e

CHARACTER CHECK: What does it mean to be loyal?

PLACE STICKER HERE

Write the missing numbers in each fact family.

1. Family: 2, 6, 8

   6 + ☐ = 8

   2 + 6 = ☐

   8 − ☐ = 2

   8 − 2 = ☐

2. Family: 3, 7, 10

   7 + ☐ = 10

   3 + 7 = ☐

   10 − 3 = ☐

   10 − ☐ = 7

Look at the spinner. Answer the questions.

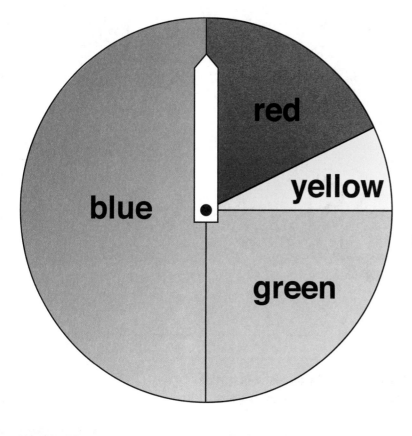

3. What color will the spinner probably land on most often?

   _____

4. What color will the spinner probably land on least often?

   _____

DAY 16

Say each word. Listen for the long *o* sound. Draw Xs on the two words that do not have the long *o* sound.

hose	note	joke	bone
rose	page	poke	side
toad	boat	roast	goat
cone	toast	soap	soak

Say the name of each picture. Write the letters you hear to spell each word.

5.

___ ___ a ___

6.

___ ___ a ___

7.

___ ___ a ___ ___

8.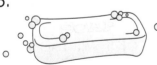

___ ___ a ___

9.

___ ___ ___ e

10.

___ ___ ___ e

FACTOID: A paleontologist is a scientist who studies fossils and dinosaur bones.

PLACE STICKER HERE

Circle the number in each set that is more.
EXAMPLE:

(26) or 15	1. 70 or 71	2. 25 or 15
3. 59 or 60	4. 9 or 11	5. 87 or 69

Circle the number in each set that is less.
EXAMPLE:

63 or (36)	6. 45 or 38	7. 12 or 21
8. 30 or 50	9. 90 or 93	10. 28 or 42

Use the letters in the box to see how many words you can make. You will use each letter more than once.

b	m	n	p	r	s	t

p an	___at	___in
___an	___at	___in
___an	___at	___ug
___an	___at	___ug
___ut	___et	___op
___ut	___et	___op

DAY 17

Say each word. Listen for the long _u_ sound. Draw Xs on the two words that do not have the long _u_ sound.

cute	tune	fume	unit
tire	mule	fuse	cube
beach	mute	tube	juice

Say the name of each picture. Write the letter sounds you hear to spell each word.

11.

___ ___ ___ e

12.

___ ___ ___ e

13.

___ ___ ___ e

14.

___ ___ ___ ___ c

 FITNESS FLASH: Jog in place for 30 seconds.

* See page ii.

PLACE STICKER HERE

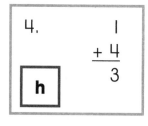

DAY 18

Check the answers. Draw Xs on the boxes with incorrect sums. To solve the riddle, write the leftover letters in order on the answer lines.

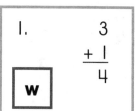

1.
```
    3
  + 1
    4
```
w

2.
```
    2
  + 2
    6
```
r

3.
```
    0
  + 2
    2
```
a

4.
```
    1
  + 4
    3
```
h

5.
```
    1
  + 1
    2
```
v

6.
```
    1
  + 2
    5
```
m

7.
```
    0
  + 1
    1
```
e

8.
```
    4
  + 1
    5
```
s

How can you tell that the ocean is friendly?

It ____ ____ ____ ____ ____ .

Count the money in each hand. Write the total amount.

9.

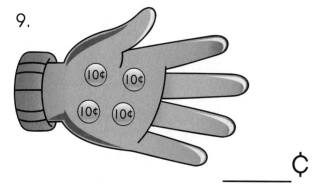

____ ¢

10.

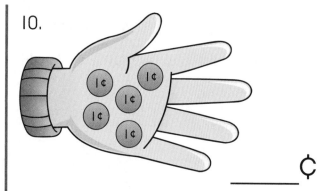

____ ¢

11.

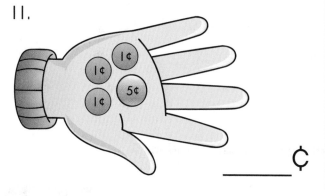

____ ¢

12.

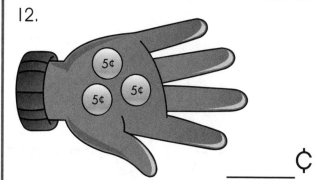

____ ¢

DAY 18

Read the story. Answer the questions.

Twins

Sara and Sasha are twins. They like to do a lot of
the same things. They both like to swim, jump rope,
and ride bikes.

But, even twins like to do different things. Sara likes to play softball. Sasha
likes to dance. In the winter, Sara likes to ice-skate. Sasha likes to go
sledding. To help at home, Sara likes to set the table.
Sasha likes to sweep the floor.

Both girls think that it is fun to have a twin.

13. Sara and Sasha are _____.

    A. twins

    B. friends

    C. teammates

14. Do the girls like being twins? _____

15. Draw a line to match each girl to the activities that she likes.

                          ice-skating

        Sara   sweeping the floor

                          sledding

        Sasha   dancing

                          setting the table

                          playing softball

FACTOID: Twenty-two percent of twins are left-handed.

PLACE
STICKER
HERE

Look at each clock. Write the time shown.

1.

2.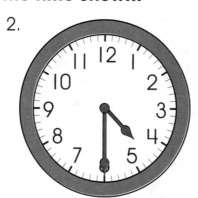

3.

1. ___:___
2. ___:___
3. ___:___

Read the time below each clock. Draw hands to show the correct time.

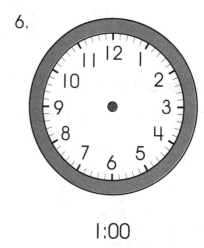

4.

5.

6.

11:30

6:00

1:00

Pillowcase Race

Ask an adult if you may use an old pillowcase, pillows, and couch cushions. Use the soft objects to set up a winding course. Mark a turnaround spot so that you can retrace your hops to the start of the course.

Step into the pillowcase and hop as fast as you can around the course. Ask an adult to time you. Set a goal and repeat the course to try to beat your time. Keep trying until you reach your goal or show improvement.

* See page ii.

DAY 19

Say the name of each picture. Circle the two pictures in each row that have the same long vowel sound.

7.

8.

9.

Number the pictures in the order in which they happened.

 FITNESS FLASH: Hop on your left foot 10 times.

* See page ii.

PLACE STICKER HERE

136

© Carson-Dellosa

Have an adult help you measure your height and weight again. Fill in the blanks. Compare these measurements to your measurements on page 3. Then, draw and color the picture to look like you.

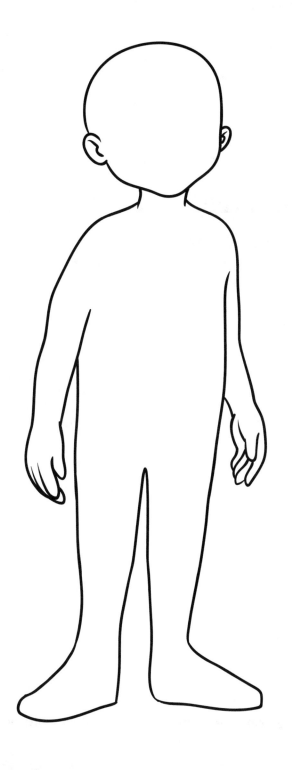

Your Height:

_____

Your Weight:

_____

How much have you grown this summer?

_____

DAY 20

Say the name of each picture. Circle the number that tells how many syllables are in each name.

1.    1   2

2.    1   2

3.    1   2

Say the name of the first picture. Change the first letter to make a new word that names the second picture. Write the new word on the line.

4. king  _____

5.  sail  _____

6.  cap   _____

CHARACTER CHECK: Write three positive things that you like about yourself.

© Carson-Dellosa

PLACE STICKER HERE

The Magic of Mulch

Does mulch (pine needles
or leaves) help keep moisture
in soil?

Materials:
- spade
- 2 plastic storage
  containers
- potting soil
- plastic cup
- water
- mulch

Procedure:

With an adult, use the spade to fill two plastic storage containers with
the same amount of potting soil. Use the plastic cup to pour the same
amount of water over the soil in each container. Feel the soil. Cover
the soil in one container with mulch. Do not cover the soil in the second
container. Place both containers in a sunny location. Feel the soil in each
container every day for three days.

1. Which soil feels wetter on the third day? _____

   _____

2. Why is the soil in one container wetter than the soil in the other

   container? _____

3. How could a person keep the soil in her garden from drying out?

   _____

   _____

BONUS

Starting a New Tree

How do trees make more trees?

Materials:
- seeds from trees
- 2–3 disposable foam cups
- potting soil
- water
- notebook

Procedure:
Go outside with an adult. Collect seeds from trees such as maple, ash, pecan, and walnut. Have an adult help you add potting soil to each cup. Bury a few seeds in each cup. Water lightly. Place the cups on a windowsill. Water the soil regularly so that it is moist but not wet. Look each day for growing seedlings. Record the dates and your observations in the notebook.

1. If you continued to water and care for your seedlings, what would

   they grow into? _____

2. How do seeds move from one place to another? Circle all of the

   correct answers.

   A. Wind blows the seeds from one place to another.

   B. Seeds fall and stick to people and animals.

   C. The seeds walk themselves from one place to another.

   D. Rain moves the seeds from one place to another.

* See page ii.

Heroes

Who is your hero? Read about this person online. Answer the questions. Draw a picture of this person in the box.

Name: _____

Born in:_____

What do you like or admire about

this person? _____

_____

_____

_____

_____

_____

What would you like to talk about with this person? _____

_____

_____

_____

_____

Road Signs

A person riding a bike must observe many road signs and signals in order to stay safe. Ask an adult to play the Road Signs game with you.

With an adult, find an example on the Internet of each road sign or signal in the chart below. Print the examples in a size that is large enough to easily be seen from a distance. Then, review the chart and printed examples. Begin the game when you are familiar with each sign or signal and the action associated with it.

Buckle your helmet securely for safety. When you are ready, ask an adult to display the "green light" signal. Pretend to ride your bike by holding imaginary handlebars while jogging forward.

The adult will display each traffic sign or signal. When the sign changes, perform its action from the chart. Remember to obey the speed limit and all traffic signs and signals. Otherwise, you might get a ticket!

Sign or Signal	Action
Green light	Jog slowly forward.
Left turn sign	Turn in circles to the left.
Left turn signal	Hold your left arm straight out. Then, turn to the left.
One way	Drive only in the direction in which the arrow points.
Red light	Come to a complete stop.
Right turn sign	Turn in circles to the right.
Right turn signal	Hold your left arm out in an *L* shape with your hand up. Then, turn to the right.
Slippery when wet	Slip and slide around the room.
Stoplight	Come to a complete stop.
Stop sign	Come to a complete stop.
Stop signal	Hold your left arm out in an *L* shape with your hand down. Then, stop.
Yield	Slow down and watch for other traffic.

* See page ii.

Mayflower Soap Ship

In September 1620, Pilgrims sailed from England across the Atlantic Ocean. They sailed on the *Mayflower* hoping to reach the New World. After landing in what is now the United States, they established the colony of Plymouth.

Materials:
- construction paper
- toothpicks
- floating bath soap
- water
- scissors
- tape
- sink

Procedure: Have an adult cut several rectangles from construction paper. Each rectangle should be about the same size as the bar of soap. These will be the "sails." Tape a toothpick to each sail. Press each toothpick into the bar of soap to make a ship.

Fill the sink with water. Carefully place your boat in the water. Blow gently on the sails to move your ship across the water. Think about a new land that your ship could sail to.

Draw a picture of your ship.

BONUS

Take It Outside!

Decorate an empty shoe box to make a "treasure chest." Fill the box with "treasure." Go outside with an adult and hide your treasure chest. Think of three clues about the location of the treasure chest. See if a friend or family member can follow your clues to find the treasure chest. Remember to bring your treasure chest inside at the end of the day.

Look around your house and list in a notebook five colors that you see. Go outside with an adult. Take your list with you and find items that match the colors on your list. Write the names of the items next to their colors.

Go outside with an adult during a rain shower. Stand under an overhang. Watch the raindrops hit the ground. What shapes do raindrops make when they hit the ground? What else do you notice about the falling rain? Write or draw your observations in a notebook.

* See page ii.

Section 1

Day 2: Students should trace and write the numbers.; Students should trace the lines to connect the fish and fishbowl, dog and doghouse, and bee and beehive.

Students should practice writing the letter *B*.; Students should circle the book, bell, and butterfly.

Day 3: Students should trace and write the numbers.; Students should circle the following shapes:

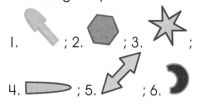

Students should practice writing the letter *C*.; Students should circle the can, cat, car, and carrot.

Day 4: Students should trace and write the numbers.; Students should complete the shapes as shown:

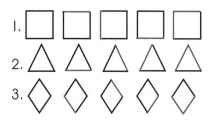

Students should practice writing the letter *D*.; Students should circle the doll, desk, dime, and dog.

Day 5: Students should color the following number

of boxes: horse–1; goat–2; sheep–3; hen–5; cat–6.

Students should practice writing the letter *F*.; Students should circle the fence, fire truck, feather, and fan.

Day 6:

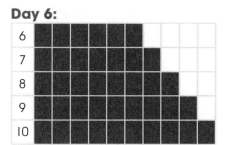

Students should write the following lowercase letters: c, d, f, h, j, l, m, p, r, s, t, w, x, y.

Students should practice writing the letter *G*.; Students should circle the gum, goat, guitar, and gate.

Day 7: 1. 6; 2. 7; 3. 8; 4. 10; Students should write the following uppercase letters: C, D, F, G, I, J, K, L, N, O, P, R, T, U, V, X, Y.

Students should practice writing the letter *H*.; Students should circle the house, hand, hat, and helicopter.

Day 8: 1.–4. Students should draw and color the correct number of shapes.; Students should draw the following shapes:

5. ⬤ ; 6. ◯ ; 7. ▲

Students should practice writing the letter *J*.; Students should circle the jar, jet,

jack-o'-lantern, and jelly beans.

Day 9: Students should color the five circles red. Students should color the three squares blue.; Students should match each uppercase letter to its lowercase letter.

Students should practice writing the letter *K*.; Students should circle the king, key, kite, and koala.

Day 10: Students should color the four triangles yellow. Students should color the four rectangles green.; Students should match each uppercase letter to its lowercase letter.

Students should practice writing the letter *L*.; Students should circle the ladder, lamp, leaf, and lemon.

Day 11: 1. 9; 2. 4; 3. 16; 4. 20; Students should complete the graph as shown:

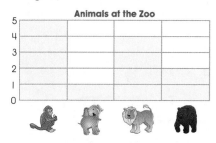

5. monkeys

Students should practice writing the letter *M*.; Students should circle the mop, monkey, mailbox, and mitten.

Day 12: I. 1; 2. 5; 3. 11; 4. 18; Students should circle the goat. Students should draw a rectangle around the sheep. Students should draw a triangle around the chicken.

Students should practice writing the letter *N*.; Students should circle the net, nuts, notebook, and nine.

Day 13: Starting from the left, students should color the first race car blue, the second race car green, and the third race car orange.; Students should circle the girl and the baby. Students should draw Xs on the school and the farm. Students should draw squares around the pencil and the desk.

Students should practice writing the letter *P*.; Students should circle the penguin, pumpkin, pencil, and piano.

Day 14: I. Students should circle the top-right fishbowl.; 2. Students should circle the top-right plate.; Students should complete the maze as shown:

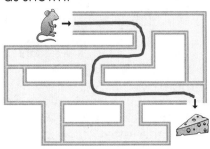

Students should practice writing the letter *Q*.; Students should circle the quilt,

question mark, quail, and quarter.

Day 15: Students should circle the following sets: I. five strawberries; 2. two apples.

Students should practice writing the letter *R*.; Students should circle the rocket, rabbit, ring, and rainbow.

Day 16: Students should complete the graph as shown:

I	2	3	4	5
6	7	8	9	10
11	12	13	14	15
16	17	18	19	20
21	22	23	24	25

Drawings will vary.

Students should practice writing the letter *S*.; Students should circle the sock, seal, soap, sun, and saw.

Day 17: Students should number the clock.; 4:00; Students should trace and write each color word and color each picture.

Students should practice writing the letter *T*.; Students should circle the tiger, tent, top, and turtle.

Day 18: Clock times will vary.; Students should trace and write each color word and color each picture.

Students should practice writing the letter *V*.; Students

should circle the vase, van, vest, and violin.

Day 19: 9:00, 5:00, 2:00; Students should trace and write each color word and color each picture.

Students should practice writing the letter *W*.; Students should circle the window, watermelon, watch, and wagon.

Day 20: Students should complete the maze as shown:

Students should practice writing the letter *X*.; Students should circle the ox, box, X-ray, and six.

Wind Direction: I.–3. Answers will vary.

Staying Cool: I. A; 2. B; 3. Answers will vary.; 4. Drawings will vary.

Being a Good Citizen: Students should circle the first and third pictures. Drawings will vary.

Then and Now: Students should circle the cell phone, jet, TV, laptop computer, and car. Students should draw an

X on the dinosaur, quill pen, knight, and castle.

Community Helpers:

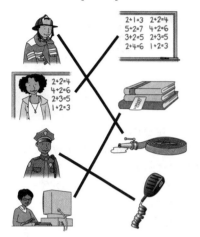

Section II

Day 1: 1. 2; 2. 4; 3. 3; 4. 4; 5. 3; 6. 5; 7. 4; 8. 5; Students should trace and color the picture.

Students should practice writing the letter *Y.*; Students should circle the yogurt, yolk, yak, and yarn.

Day 2: 1. 5; 2. 6; 3. 5; 4. 6; 5. 2; 6. 5; 7. 4; 8. 7; 9. 6; 10. 3

Students should practice writing the letter *Z.*; Students should circle the zipper, zebra, and zero.

Day 3: 1. 4; 2. 5; 3. 3; 4. 4; 5. 4; 6. 5; 7. 5; 8. 5; 9. 2; Students should color the three circles red. Students should color the three squares purple. Students should color four triangles green. Students should color the three rectangles blue.

Students should practice

writing the letter *A.*; Students should circle the apple, pan, hand, and hat.

Day 4:

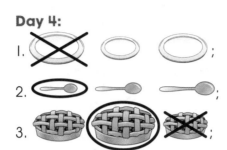

Students should trace and write each letter.

4. fan; 5. cat; 6. map; 7. van; 8. cap; Students should draw an X on the word *bed.*

Day 5: 1. tree; 2. a bone; 3. 5; 4. rat; 5. hat; 6. map; 7. bat; 8. can; 9. bag; 10. cat, ran, sat; 11. sad, rat; 12. has, hat; 13. man, has, maps

Day 6: 1. 1; 2. 1; 3. 3; 4. 3; 5. 2; 6. 0; 7. 1; 8. 2; Students should color the rainbow as shown:

Students should underline each of the following words each time the word is used: Sam, has, cat, Sam's, Max, cap, lap, bag, naps.; 9. A; 10. B; 11. A

Day 7: 1. 4; 2. 4; 3. 3; 4. 0; 5. 1; 6. 2; 7. 1; 8. 0; 9. 5; 10. 3; Students should complete each pattern as shown:

11.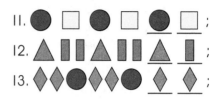

Students should practice writing the letter *E.*; Students should circle the elephant, tent, bed, nest, and bell.

Day 8: 1. 2; 2. 1; 3. 2; 4. 3; 5. 1; 6. 2; 7. 1; 8. 1; 9. 4; Students should trace and write each letter.

10. tent; 11. pen; 12. vest; 13. egg; 14. nest; Students should draw an X on the word *bag.*

Day 9: 1. 4; 2. 1; 3. 5; 4. 2; 5. 1; 6. 0; 7. 3; 8. 0; 9. 4; 10. 1; 11.–14. Students should complete each picture.

15. web; 16. net; 17. jet; 18. ten; 19. bell; 20. bed; 21. Jed, bed; 22. Peg, pet, hen; 23. Ben, Wes, jets; 24. Beth, red, pen

Day 10: Students should circle the numbers as shown:

12	21	(12)	15	(12)	51	(12)	21	(12)
96	(96)	99	66	86	(96)	66	(96)	(96)
54	55	(54)	45	43	(54)	45	(54)	52
71	(71)	17	(71)	11	(71)	(71)	17	(71)
35	53	55	(35)	(35)	33	(35)	53	(35)

Students should color the crayons.

Students should underline each of the following words each time the word is used:

Meg, vet, vets, help, pets, get, well, leg, mend, head, pep, pet.; I. B; 2. pets; 3. T, T, F

Day 11: I. 4; 2. 5; 3. 2; 4. 3; Students should practice writing their names.

Students should practice writing the letter *I*.; Students should circle the wig, ring, pin, bib, and fish.

Day 12: I. 7; 2. 5; 3. 10; 4. 12; Students should match numbers and sets as follows: I–apple, 2–oranges, 3–lemons, 4–balloons, 5–balls.

5. sink; 6. milk; 7. bib; 8. ship; 9. six; Students should draw an X on the word *bug*.

Day 13: I. Students should circle the sandwich on the left.; 2. Students should circle the middle carrot.; 3. Students should circle the bean on the right.; 4. Students should circle the top-right eraser.; 5. Students should circle the last cat.; 6. Students should circle the third dog.; 7. Students should circle the second fish.

8. fish; 9. ring; 10. pin; II. six; 12. wig; 13. lips; 14. Jim, hid, bib, in; 15. fish, swim, in; 16. big, did, flip; 17. Jill, will, swim

Day 14: I. 7; 2. 4; Students should match the numbers and sets as follows: 6–erasers, 7–heads of lettuce, 8–pies, 9–baseballs,

10–party horns.

Students should practice writing the letter *O*.; Students should circle the lock, clock, sock, and frog.

Day 15: I. ball; 2. book; 3. pumpkin; 4. shoe; Students should complete the crossword puzzles as shown:

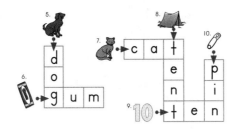

II. clock; 12. lock; 13. sock; 14. top; 15. rock; Students should draw an X on the word *bib*.

Day 16: I. Students should circle the pitcher.; 2. Students should circle the gift on the left.; 3. Students should circle the box on the right.; 4. Students should circle the vase on the right.; Students should match the pictures as shown:

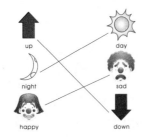

5. jog; 6. dog; 7. box; 8. mop; 9. fox; 10. frog; II. frog, hop, on, top, box; 12. dog, fox, pond; 13. John, box, rock; 14. Tom, jog

Day 17: Answers will vary but may include:

Students should underline each of the following words each time the word is used: frog, on, log, pond, along, dog, Rob, song, hopped, off, fox, popped.; I. Rob the dog; 2. C; 3. It hopped; 4. It popped; 5. Answers will vary.

Day 18: I. in; 2. over; Students should circle the words as shown:

Students should practice writing the letter *U*.; Students should circle the duck, mug, rug, and bus.

Day 19: Students should touch and say each number.

I. rug; 2. duck; 3. sun; 4. tub; 5. mug; Students should draw an X on the word *hat*.

Day 20: Students should skip count to connect the following numbers: I. 0, 2, 4, 6, 8, 10; 2. 12, 14, 16, 18, 20.; 3. Wednesday; 4. Thursday; 5. July 8; 6. Friday 7. sun; 8. gum; 9. bus; 10. rug; II. duck;

12. nut; 13. lucky, duck; 14. cut, bud; 15. Gus, gum, bus; 16. Judd, mud, rug

Constellations: 1. Answers will vary.; 2. at night; 3. Answers will vary but may include: other planets, the moon, man-made satellites, and comets.

Grasping Objects: 1. B; 2. A; 3. monkey, gorilla

It's Only Natural!: 1. N; 2. N; 3. M; 4. N; 5. M; 6. M; 7. N; 8. M; 9. M; 10. M

Globe: The globe should be colored as shown:

Travel Today: Drawings will vary.

Section III

Day 1: 1. 5; 2. 5; 3. 7; 4. 3; 5. 7; 6. 1; 7. 2; 8. 4; 9. 1; 10. 3; Students should complete the table as shown:

1	2	3	4	5	6	7	8	9	10
11	12	13	14	15	16	17	18	19	20
21	22	23	24	25	26	27	28	29	30
31	32	33	34	35	36	37	38	39	40
41	42	43	44	45	46	47	48	49	50

11. B; 12. C; 13. Answers will vary but may include: pups, cubs, run, tug, and much.

Day 2: 1. 5; 2. 6; 3. 4; 4. 3; Students should complete the table as shown:

51	52	53	54	55	56	57	58	59	60
61	62	63	64	65	66	67	68	69	70
71	72	73	74	75	76	77	78	79	80
81	82	83	84	85	86	87	88	89	90
91	92	93	94	95	96	97	98	99	100

5. fish, feather; 6. camera, cake; 7. desk, dog; 8. goat, guitar; 9. hat, hammer

Day 3: Students should write the following numbers: 4, 6, 8, 12, 14, 18, 20, 22, 24, 26, 28.

1. seal, sock; 2. net, nail; 3. pear, pie; 4. tent, turtle; 5. bell, bed

Day 4: Students should write the following numbers: 5, 10, 15, 20, 25, 30, 35, 40, 45, 50; Drawings will vary.

1. jar, jet; 2. rabbit, ring; 3. key, kite; 4. web, watch; 5. zebra, zipper

Day 5: 1. 20; 2. 10; 3. 15; 4. 25; 5. hat, rat; 6. can, pan; 7. top, mop

8. A; 9. B; 10. B; 11. She keeps the animals safe and happy. She cleans the habitats and gives the animals food and water.

Day 6: Students should complete the table as shown:

10	20	30	40	50
60	70	80	90	100

Students should draw a house and color both pictures.

1. z; 2. k; 3. r; 4. l; 5. d; 6. t; 7. w

Day 7: 1. 20; 2. 60; 3. 30; 4. 40; Answers will vary but may include: 25 pennies; 5 nickels; 1 dime and 3 nickels; 2 dimes and 5 pennies; 1 dime and 15 pennies; 1 dime, 2 nickels, and 5 pennies. 5. s; 6. d; 7. f; 8. p; 9. l; 10. y; 11. v

Day 8: 1. 8; 2. 9; 3. 10; 4. 9; 5. 7; 6. 10; 7. 9; 8. 9; 9. 10; 10. 7; 11. 8; 12. 8; Students should connect the dots as shown:

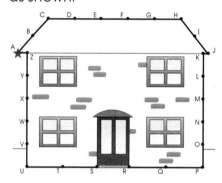

13. B; 14. B; 15. I, high, fly, by; 16. Answers will vary.

Day 9: 1. 8; 2. 6; 3. 7; 4. 8; 5. 10; 6. 9; 7. 8; 8. 10; 9. 9; 10. 9; 11. 10; 12. 9; Students should circle the words as shown:

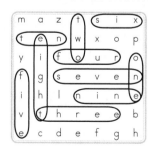

13. n; 14. g; 15. k; 16. p; 17. x; 18. l; 19. r; 20. f; 21. d; 22. b; 23. m

Day 10: 1. 4; 2. 3; 3. 8; 4. 4; 5. 1; 6. 5; 7. 3; 8. 1; 9. 3; 10. 2; 11. 5; 12. 2; Drawings will vary.

13. m; 14. t; 15. g; 16. p; 17. x; 18. l; 19. n

Day 11: 1. 3; 2. 6; 3. 9; 4. 3; 5. 4; 6. 3; 7. 4; 8. 8; 9. 4; 10. 4; 11. 0; 12. 3; 13. 10; 14. 2; 15. 2; Students should match the following pictures: box–fox; top–mop; frog–log; pan–fan.

16. w, g; 17. m, g; 18. t, p; 19. b, x; 20. d, g; 21. t or b, b; 22. v, n

Day 12: 1. 10; 2. 6; 3. 4; 4. 8; 5. 8; 6. 9; 7. 3; 8. 1; 9. 10; 10. 2; 11. 5; 12. 2; 13. Students should circle the car and star.; 14. Students should circle the key and bee.; 15. Students should circle the moon and spoon.

16. C; 17. B; 18. pancakes and juice; 19. played tag and hide-and-seek.

Day 13: 1. 2; 2. 4; 3. 6; 4. 8; 5. 10, 6. 0; 7. 0; 8. 0; 9. 0; 10. 0; 11. 0; 12. 0; Drawings will vary.

Students should draw Xs on the words *tire* and *boat*.; 13. cake; 14. tape; 15. vase; 16. nail; 17. rain; 18. paint or pails

Day 14: 1. 6; 2. 10; 3. 8; 4. 9; 5. 6; 6. 2; 7. 9; 8. 3; 9. 9; 10. 5; 11. 5; 12. 4; 13. 9; 14. 1; 15. 9; 16. 3 – 1 = 2 balloons;

17. 5 – 3 = 2 bees

Students should draw Xs on the words *rose* and *rake*.; 18. tree; 19. three; 20. feet; 21. peach; 22. leaf; 23. peas

Day 15: 1. 10; 2. 11; 3. 13; 4. 14; 5. 12; 6. 15

Students should draw Xs on the words *cute* and *seed*.; 7. kite; 8. pie; 9. slide; 10. five; 11. bike; 12. nine

Day 16: 1. 2, 8, 6, 6; 2. 3, 10, 7, 3; 3. blue; 4. yellow

Students should draw Xs on the words *page* and *side*.; 5. boat; 6. goat; 7. toast; 8. soap; 9. note; 10. rose

Day 17: 1. 71; 2. 25; 3. 60; 4. 11; 5. 87; 6. 38; 7. 12; 8. 30; 9. 90; 10. 28; Answers will vary but may include: ran, tan, man, rut, but, put, nut, rat, sat, bat, mat, pat, set, bet, pet, net, tin, bin, pin, rug, tug, bug, mug, top, mop, pop.

Students should draw Xs on the words *tire* and *beach*.; 11. mule; 12. tube; 13. cube; 14. music

Day 18: Students should draw an X on the following problems: 2, 4, and 6; It waves; 9. 40; 10. 5; 11. 8; 12. 15

13. A; 14. yes; 15. Sara–ice skating, setting the table, playing softball; Sasha–sweeping the floor, sledding, dancing

Day 19: 1. 2:00; 2. 4:30; 3. 10:00; Students should complete the clocks as shown:

7. tree, bee; 8. goat, bone; 9. vase, cake; 1, 3, 2, 4

Day 20: Answers and drawings will vary.; 1. 2; 2. 1; 3. 2; 4. ring; 5. tail; 6. map

The Magic of Mulch:
1. The one with the mulch feels wetter.; 2. The mulch kept the soil from drying out.; 3. She could cover the soil with mulch.

Starting a New Tree: 1. trees; 2. A, B, D

Heroes: Answers and drawings will vary.

Mayflower Soap Ship: Drawings will vary.

Aa

Bb

Cc

Dd

Ee

Ff

Gg

Hh

Ii

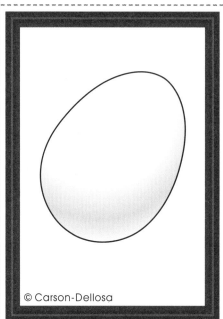

Jj	Kk	Ll
© Carson-Dellosa	© Carson-Dellosa	© Carson-Dellosa
Mm	Nn	Oo
© Carson-Dellosa	© Carson-Dellosa	© Carson-Dellosa
Pp	Qq	Rr
© Carson-Dellosa	© Carson-Dellosa	© Carson-Dellosa

© Carson-Dellosa

© Carson-Dellosa

© Carson-Dellosa

© Carson-Dellosa

© Carson-Dellosa

© Carson-Dellosa

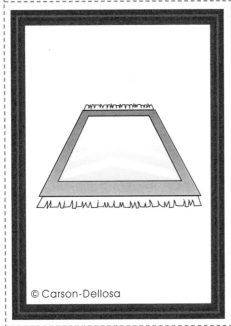

© Carson-Dellosa

© Carson-Dellosa

© Carson-Dellosa

Ss	Tt	Uu
© Carson-Dellosa	© Carson-Dellosa	© Carson-Dellosa
Vv	Ww	Xx
© Carson-Dellosa	© Carson-Dellosa	© Carson-Dellosa
Yy	Zz	O
© Carson-Dellosa	© Carson-Dellosa	© Carson-Dellosa

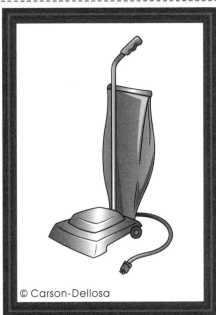

zero

1	2	3
© Carson-Dellosa	© Carson-Dellosa	© Carson-Dellosa
4	5	6
© Carson-Dellosa	© Carson-Dellosa	© Carson-Dellosa
7	8	9
© Carson-Dellosa	© Carson-Dellosa	© Carson-Dellosa

three	two	one
© Carson-Dellosa	© Carson-Dellosa	© Carson-Dellosa
six	five	four
© Carson-Dellosa	© Carson-Dellosa	© Carson-Dellosa
nine	eight	seven
© Carson-Dellosa	© Carson-Dellosa	© Carson-Dellosa

© Carson-Dellosa

3:00	2:00	1:00
© Carson-Dellosa	© Carson-Dellosa	© Carson-Dellosa
6:00	5:00	4:00
© Carson-Dellosa	© Carson-Dellosa	© Carson-Dellosa
9:00	8:00	7:00
© Carson-Dellosa	© Carson-Dellosa	© Carson-Dellosa

© Carson-Dellosa

© Carson-Dellosa

© Carson-Dellosa

1¢

© Carson-Dellosa

5¢

© Carson-Dellosa

10¢

© Carson-Dellosa

25¢

© Carson-Dellosa

+

© Carson-Dellosa

−

© Carson-Dellosa

12:00	11:00	10:00
© Carson-Dellosa	© Carson-Dellosa	© Carson-Dellosa
dime	nickel	penny
© Carson-Dellosa	© Carson-Dellosa	© Carson-Dellosa
minus	plus	quarter
© Carson-Dellosa	© Carson-Dellosa	© Carson-Dellosa

© Carson-Dellosa

© Carson-Dellosa

© Carson-Dellosa

© Carson-Dellosa

© Carson-Dellosa

© Carson-Dellosa

© Carson-Dellosa

© Carson-Dellosa

© Carson-Dellosa

less than	greater than	equals
© Carson-Dellosa	© Carson-Dellosa	© Carson-Dellosa
triangle	square	circle
© Carson-Dellosa	© Carson-Dellosa	© Carson-Dellosa
oval	rhombus	rectangle
© Carson-Dellosa	© Carson-Dellosa	© Carson-Dellosa

The Original

Summer Bridge Activities™

Congratulations!

This certifies that

_____

Name

has completed **Summer Bridge Activities™**.

_____

Parent's Signature

www.carsondellosa.com